NO EASY ROAD

INSPIRATIONAL THOUGHTS ON PRAYER

DICK EASTMAN

BAKER BOOK HOUSE • Grand Rapids, Michigan

PREFACE

Facing frustrations of an uncertain future I pondered thoughts of never preaching again. My throat became progressively worse and doctors offered no medical solution. I left the pulpit for several months, discouraged. My ministry seriously suffered. Even soft conversation in counseling situations caused severe pain in my throat. At twenty-five years of age I was confused. Why would such a thing occur in my youth?

Nights were long as I sat alone weeping before God. Future plans developed in my thinking. I reasoned, "Africa's the place to go. My experience with the printing press could be the foundation for a life-long literature ministry"

But God's plan differed. It became obvious He had an important lesson to teach me. Prayer was the topic and the closet became the classroom.

After extensive research *NO EASY ROAD* resulted. I believe these important thoughts on prayer are essential to productive living. Prayer, to this writer, is the crux of Christian commitment. We would call it the voice of Christianity or the throat of the Church. It was prayer that ultimately restored this writer's throat and I believe prayer will ultimately restore needed power to the Church.

But the going will be strenuous. Persistence is prerequisite. Expect setbacks but refuse retreat. Prayer is a difficult endeavor. The road to heaven is often obscured by myriad obstacles. Those interested in conquering rugged prayer heights will find challenge and guidance in *NO EASY ROAD*.

Dick Eastman

INTRODUCTION

Recently, while sitting thoughtfully in a quiet roadside restaurant, I made a startling discovery. With pen and scratch paper, I arrived at some most amazing figures concerning our potential as Christians to reach every being on Planet Earth with the good news about Jesus Christ.

First, I calculated the number of new converts that were being won to Christ daily by the fastest-growing evangelical denomination at that time, according to a religious census. The report explained how this particular organization was winning 1500 new converts to Christ daily.

Another report, from an international Bible distribution ministry, explained that 2 billion people had never heard the message of Jesus even one time. At the rate of 1500 per day it would require over 3000 years to reach everyone on earth, and even that accomplishment would require zero population growth. Of course, it would take much longer if the population continued to double every twenty to thirty years. And even all denominational efforts together would fall far short of the goal.

Suddenly I was struck with the futility of the challenge of Christ to reach every person in the world. Like so many Christians, I almost determined that the task was not possible, especially if our Lord should return a second time before the year 2000.

But then I inwardly quizzed myself, "Would Christ command us to do that which is not possible?" My heart answer was quick in coming: "Certainly not." There must, therefore, be a way to fulfill the command of Christ literally and effectively. And, I reasoned, whatever that method is, it will certainly necessitate a miracle; indeed, a miracle of such unprecedented magnitude that it lingers well beyond the realm of our finest imagination. Yes, my heart cried out, it will take a real miracle, a supernatural missionary miracle that will come only through intercessory prayer.

Beloved reader, my heart leaps for joy as I declare that the means to reach the goal of world evangelism is not a dream but a reality. All we need now is the power behind that means. The means is massive, systematic distribution of the gospel message to every place of shelter for human beings who dwell on earth. World Literature Crusade is doing exactly this with astounding results. W.L.C. is now actively working with an amazing 415 denominations and evangelistic organizations to fulfill the Great Commission of Jesus Christ literally. In recent days as many as 72,000 decisions for Christ have been mailed into W.L.C. offices around the world in a single month.

Accurate documentation further reveals that gospel messages distributed through W.L.C. now daily reach the homes of more than 1,000,000 people. At such a rate the entire world could be reached in the next twelve years, provided all 210 countries of the world were open to such intense distribution. Several are not and the prospects for change are bleak. Here is where prayer power is needed. Dr. Jack McAlister, founder and president of World Literature Crusade, is quick to declare that prayer is the single most important force behind the impact of this successful missionary organization. Further, according to the Reverend McAlister, the only possible hope for fulfilling the Great Commission of Jesus lies in the dedicated laborers who systematically place the gospel in every home in the world—backed hourly by the greatest prayer force in the history of the human race. I invite you to join that force.

Daily this army will lift all 210 countries of the world in intercessory prayer. (See the appendix for suggestions as to how you can begin a prayer ministry in your own home). To share insights into prayer, I invite the reader on a journey to power, along the road of intercession. After taking the journey, pass this book on to another or write World Literature Crusade for extra copies. Ask W.L.C. for the new World Prayer Map, showing every country on earth, as well as supplying helpful prayer information. Together, let us call the world to prayer.

Dick Eastman

The author of *No Easy Road* has prepared a special three-month course on prayer that is presently available on cassette. The course, based on *No Easy Road,* is suitable for personal use or in home study or church groups. A complete instructor's guide is also available. For information on the study write:

World Literature Crusade
P. O. Box 1313
Studio City, CA 91604

CONTENTS

NO EASY ROAD

The Christian's Journey on the Road of Prayer

Oh, ye who sigh and languish
    And mourn your lack of power,
Hear ye this gentle whisper:
    "Could ye not watch one hour?"
For fruitfulness and blessing
    There is no royal road;
The power for holy service
    Is intercourse with God.

1 NO EASY ROAD

A Communist editor confessed, "The Gospel is a much more powerful weapon for the renovation of society than our Marxist view. Yet it is we who shall conquer you in the end. We Communists do not play with words. We are realists, and because we are determined to reach our end, we also know how to provide necessary means."

Speaking of sacrifice, he said, "Of our salaries and wages we keep only what is absolutely necessary and the rest we give for propaganda purposes. To this same propaganda we also devote leisure time and part of our vacation. You, however, give only a little time and scarcely any money for the spreading of Christ's Gospel."

The angry editor then sneered, "How can anyone believe in the all-surpassing value of this Gospel if you do not practice it, if you do not spread it, if you sacrifice neither your time nor your money for that purpose? Believe me, it is we who shall conquer, because we believe in our Communist gospel and are willing to sacrifice everything, even life itself. But you, you are afraid of soiling your hands."

Perhaps this Communist editor was accurate in his conclusion. Many seek an easy Christianity in this age of affluence. The Christian life, however, is not an easy road.

Rather, it is a challenging journey demanding much of its travelers. Daily we strive in hopeful anticipation for tne prize before us. Paul testifies, "I press toward the mark for the prize . . ." (Philippians 3:14).

A most vital but extremely difficult element of the Christian life is prayer. F. J. Huegel writes, "Prayer is work of such a sublime order that it lies beyond the imagination of men." E. M. Bounds emphasizes, "Prayer is not a little habit pinned on to us while we were tied to our mother's apron strings; neither is it a little decent quarter of a minute's grace said over an hour's dinner, but it is a most serious work of our most serious years." This great pray-er adds, "Spiritual work is taxing work, and men are loath to do it. Praying, true praying, costs an outlay of serious attention and of time, which flesh and blood do not relish."

Price of prayer

Relating incidents of the closing days of John Hyde, India's great pray-er, a friend told of the time when his health declined. Deeply concerned, the friend insisted Hyde visit a doctor. Later the physician said: "His heart is in an awful condition. I have never had such a serious case. The heart has shifted from its normal position to the right side. Because of stress and strain it is in such terrible condition that months of strictly quiet life will be required to bring the heart back to anything like its normal state." What caused this rare condition? Praying Hyde's friend says, "We who knew him, knew the cause: his life of incessant prayers day and night, prayers accompanied by exceedingly many tears for his converts, for his fellow-laborers, for his friends, and for the church in India."

Prayer, genuine prayer, has its price. Praying Hyde lost health but gained results few attain in this life. Even after a physician's examination, John Hyde retired to a night of prayer. This turbulent century of social and political problems cries for another man of prayer power like Hyde. One Hyde working at prayer could revolutionize the world. Truly God's pray-ers are societies' best revolutionaries.

Prayer indeed is work. But even more, prayer is an art requiring constant cultivation. Charles Spurgeon declared, "Prayer itself is an art which only the Holy Ghost can teach us. He is the giver of all prayer. Pray for prayer — pray till you can pray."

To learn prayer men must pray. We learn prayer's deepest depths in prayer, not from books. We reach prayer's highest heights in prayer, not from sermons. The only place to learn prayer, is in prayer, bent and broken on our knees. Prayer is skill developed through experience. Learning to pray is like learning a trade. We are apprentices and must serve time at it. Consistent care, thought, practice, and time are needed to become a skillful pray-er.

Great men pray

The Road of Prayer, though tough and rugged, was well-traveled by those who reached spiritual heights. Samuel Rutherford accomplished immeasurable amounts of work for Christ. What was his secret? He rose each morning at three o'clock to converse with God. Scotland's quiet night air was ladened with anguished cries penetrating the darkness as John Welch prayed. Once he remarked his day was ill spent if he could not stay eight or ten hours in secret solitude. It is said of the distinguished and effective Bishop Andrews that he spent more than five hours daily in prayer and Bible study. Charles Simeon rose each day from his bunk to bow on bended knees from four to eight. Martin Luther proclaimed prayer a saintly work of grave necessity. He confessed, "If I fail to spend two hours in prayer each morning, the devil gets the victory through the day. I have so much business I cannot get on without spending three hours daily in prayer."

Although John Wesley's life epitomized work, he gave his best hours to prayer. His motto: "The world is my parish." How did he achieve such saintly goals? He never traveled less than 4,500 miles annually, often as much as 8,000 miles in a single year. From age thirty-six he traveled Methodist circuits, riding over 225,000 miles, preaching over 40,000 sermons. He often spoke to crowds of 20,000 without benefit of modern audio equipment.

Weather never seemed to trouble Wesley. When rain fell in torrents or bitter frost gripped frozen ground, his work continued. His sermons often lasted several hours. But behind every mile and every sermon was a prayer, and backing every word, a tear. Wesley's spiritual strength was gained through someone's faithful prayer.

Most remember the Wesley brothers' triumph and splendor, but overlook the value of a mother's prayers. While John and Charles held crusades she labored on calloused knees. Unfortunately, we have no record of others who fasted and prayed for the Wesleys. Many worked as hard as these evangelists who preached and sang their way to Christian fame. No one cheered the labors of these silent servants. Few, if any, knew they contributed to the Wesleys' spiritual impact. But mark one fact and mark it clearly: behind the saving grace for every soul was someone praying.

Whosoever will may pray

The Road of Prayer may be traveled by all willing to pay the price. Preaching is the exclusive task of preachers. The missionary's task is not for everyone. But anyone can pray! One may lack talent for doing great things, as men count greatness, but one's station in life does not determine greatness in the sight of God. He looks for dedicated hearts carrying prayerful burdens. God longs for those who work at prayer. His Word declares, ". . . the effectual fervent prayer of a righteous man availeth much" (James 5:16). In other words, "He who is in good standing with God and works at prayer will see much done."

In the excellent book, *The Kneeling Christian,* the author says, "Of all the millions in India living in the bondage of Hinduism, none may pray except the Brahmins! A millionaire merchant of any other caste must get a Brahmin — often a mere boy at school — to say his prayers for him. The Muslim cannot pray unless he has learned a few phrases in Arabic, for his god hears only prayers offered in what they believe to be the holy language."

Imagine the bondage Muslims must experience when urgent needs arise. Consider the limitations placed on their prayer lives. Thank God, no limits restrict kneeling Christians. Nothing prevents our kneeling this moment, walking through sparkling gates of heaven, down shining streets of gold, and into the holiest of holies to stand in God's sweet presence. Thank God, whosoever will may pray.

Obstacles on The Road of Prayer

Abundant distractions and seemingly overwhelming obstacles plague Christians who would make progress on the Road of Prayer. At the end of the road lies the prize, the unleashing of God's sustaining power to all who have made the arduous journey. Tragically few ever reach God's place of power. Few will pay the price of work and dedication. It has been said, "The lazy man does not, will not, cannot pray, for prayer demands energy." Because many lack spiritual energy, few conquer these obstacles on the road to prayer.

Beyond the spiraling *Peak of Unbelief,* the first mountain to be conquered, lies *The Mountain of Sin,* hindering many prayers we pray. Next we must pick our way through an *Avalanche of Excuses,* removing them from the road to *The Peak of Habit.* We chose to cross slowly *The Plateau of Intercession,* for difficult lessons must be learned here. Next, we pause for a time in *Holiness Cove.* The road up the towering *Mountain of Self-Will* is especially arduous and our progress is slow. Then, *The Bridge of Balance* beckons. *The Mountain of Persistence* presents a real challenge. Beyond lies the rugged trail to *Burden's Outlook.* Then our goal appears: *Trail's End.* At the summit we stand awed at the power of Christ's promise ". . . ask anything in my name, I will do it." Let us move onward. Before us waits a crucial task. Beyond the obstacles, however, glows God's glory, the glory the psalmist sought: "To see thy power and glory . . ." (Psalm 63:2).

S. D. Gordon comments, "The greatest thing anyone can do for God and man is pray. It is not the only thing; but it is the chief thing. The great people of the earth today are the people who pray. I do not mean those who talk about prayer; nor those who say they believe in prayer; nor yet those who can explain about prayer; but I mean these people who take time to pray."

Glories of answered prayer linger before us this hour. Prayer is work, taxing work, with tireless and endless toil. It is no easy road! A wise poet reminds:

> There's no easy path to glory
>   There's no rosy road to fame.
> Prayer, no matter how you view it,
>   Is no simple parlor game.
> But its prizes call for fighting,
>   For endurance and for grit;
> For a rugged "I can do it"
>   And some "don't know when to quit."

2　THE PEAK OF UNBELIEF

"The atomic bomb will never go off, and I speak as an expert in explosives," Admiral Leahy predicted flatly in early 1945. No doubt this famed authority wishes he had never said these words.

"There has been a great deal said about a 3,000-mile high-angle rocket," proclaimed Dr. Vannevar Bush, a few years ago, "but in my opinion such a thing is impossible for many years." Today men walk on the moon.

The aviation pioneer, Octave Chanute, predicted "Airplanes will eventually be fast, they will be used in sport, but they are not to be thought of as commercial carriers." Today we have jumbo jets carrying hundreds daily.

Perhaps most amusing of such negative remarks was voiced by Lt. Joseph Ives in 1861, following exploration of the Grand Canyon. Ives stated abruptly, "The Grand Canyon is, of course, altogether useless. Ours has been the first, and will doubtless be the last, party of whites to visit this profitless locality."

A negative spirit sometimes permeates the minds of praying people. Often we forget that our Master said, ". . . What things soever ye desire, when ye pray, believe that ye receive them, and ye shall have them" (Mark 11:24).

A diary of answered prayer

George Müller stands as one who took Christ's words and prayerfully removed the obstacle of unbelief from his prayers. He testified, "God has never failed me! For nearly seventy years every need in connection with this work [caring for orphans] has been supplied. The orphans from the first until now have numbered nine thousand, five hundred, but they never wanted a meal. In answer to prayer $7,500,000 has been sent to me. We have needed as much as $200,000 in one year, and it has all come when needed. We have no committees, no collectors, no voting, and no endowment. All has come in answer to believing prayer."

Myriad victories fill Müller's diary because he prayed away his unbelief. Those privileged to know Müller saw sparkling faith and received encouragement. Pastor Charles R. Parsons spent a thrilling hour with Müller shortly before death claimed this great orphanage leader. Müller told him an answer to prayer had come just weeks before, when almost all supplies were gone. There were two thousand orphans to care for daily and not enough to feed one hundred.

"I called my beloved helpers together," reported Müller, "and told them, 'Pray, brethren, pray!' Immediately five hundred dollars was sent us, then a thousand, and in a few days seventy-five hundred came in. But always we have to be praying, always believing."

Parsons asked, "Have you saved any money for yourself?"

"He sat erect," declared Parsons, "and for several moments searched my face with an earnestness that seemed to penetrate my very soul. After a brief pause, during which his face was a sermon and the depths of his clear eyes flashed fire, he unbuttoned his coat and drew from his pocket an old-fashioned purse. Placing it in my hands he said quietly, 'All I am possessed of is in that purse — every penny!' "

Müller desired nothing but God. This is all Müller cared to have. He never dwelt on "negatives." Rather, he held constant confidence that God would never fail him. Müller's life became a *diary of answered prayers* because he learned to trust God.

Müller's mustard seed

On one occasion, Müller traveled to Canada for a speaking engagement. Dense fog settled upon the ocean and the uncertain vessel floated motionless on a silent sea. Soon Müller knocked anxiously on the captain's door expressing, "I must be in Toronto by Sunday." The captain quickly replied, "In no way can this vessel move without assuming great danger of colliding with another."

"I understand," said Mr. Müller, "but, in forty years of Christian service I have not failed to keep an appointment. I must be in Toronto Sunday!" He then asked the captain to join in special prayer that the fog lift. Embarrassed, the captain agreed. They knelt and Müller calmly asked God to lift the hindering fog. Somewhat intimidated, the captain said a simple prayer to please his anxious passenger. He no sooner began when Müller stopped him. He gently touched the captain's shoulder saying: "You need not pray. You do not believe."

Startled, the seafarer rose to leave the cabin with this unusual passenger. Walking out on deck, a look of sheer astonishment spread over the captain's face. The fog had completely lifted. George Müller silently stood by with a "just as I expected" look.

Tracing this life of faith to its beginning one finds it started simply. Müller's grain of mustard seed began to grow shortly after college when he quit his job to sacrificially pray, "I now depend on you, God." It was small and simple faith then. But, out of small beginnings grew faith to believe God for almost $200,000 every year. Müller's mustard seed grew to help ten thousand orphans live a healthy life.

Faith . . . as the grain of a mustard seed, Jesus declared, shall remove mountains (Matthew 17:20). Oh, that we would cultivate at least a small amount of faith. Imagine the results waiting for Christians who remove unbelief from their lives. Yet, the age in which we live seems to make this a most difficult feat. If God does not heal, we rely on doctors. If money fails to come for bills, we can always borrow from bank or friend. If mission fields close, we can always erect radio stations to broadcast the Gospel. In a materialistic, "self-oriented" society it is often easy to be caught in a spirit of unbelief.

Charles Allen, in *All Things Are Possible Through Prayer,* writes, "We believe in prayer. Then why don't we pray? The real reason is, we have nothing to pray for. We have everything we want without praying. The supreme tragedy of most people is that they want so little and they are satisfied with almost nothing."

All available power must be amassed to defeat Satan's attempts to fill us with doubts. Nothing defeats him like the prayer of faith. Wise indeed, are those who pray as Christ's disciples — "Lord, Increase our faith" (Luke 17:5).

Billy Bray, a remarkable Christian worker in England's last century, possessed this godly faith. Bray combined prayer with faith and blasted away at Satan. Addressing Satan once, he confidently mused, "What an old fool thee art now; I have been battling thee for twenty-eight years, and I have always beat thee, and I always shall." What a stunning blow to Satan. What a massive portion of unbelief's mountain must have tumbled that day.

This active faith carried Billy through his greatest trials. Once his child was extremely sick. When his wife encouraged him to get the doctor lest the child die, Billy took all the money they possessed, thirty-six cents, and hurried for the doctor. He met a poor man on the way who had lost a cow and was trying to get enough money to purchase another. The poor man's situation so touched Billy's heart that he gave him the entire sum. With no money he saw little use in securing a doctor and rather began praying. Miraculous healing soon came when this father prayed a simple prayer of faith. Satan felt again the sting of defeat.

Raincoats, watches, and fountain pens

Men like Billy Bray are few and far between. The tragedy is seen in lost and dying souls. Unbelievers who look at us often see only wavering, doubt-filled Christians. James proclaimed ". . . ask in faith, nothing wavering . . ." (James 1:6). Moffat translates this, ". . . let him ask in faith with never a doubt. . . ." True prayer, powerful prayer, is doubt-less prayer.

Rees Howells lived doubt-less faith. He became a dedicated twentieth-century intercessor, establishing orphanages and a Bible school during the trying years of World War II. In *Rees Howells: Intercessor,* a masterpiece by Norman Grubb, Howells' stirring story of doubt-less faith in action is related.

Once Mr. Howells made ready his departure for Africa as a missionary. He and his partner were ready to board a train for London to make connections with an ocean-going vessel for the lengthy journey. They had only ten shillings between them, enough to take them twenty miles on the train.

"We felt sure the money would come so we went to the platform to wait for its arrival," relates Howells. "The time for the train to depart came and we decided to go as far as possible."

Leaving the train twenty miles later, they met friends who invited them to breakfast. Surely, thought Howells, God had sent these friends to pay the way, but departure time arrived and no offers of financial aid were given.

Rees Howells testified, "The Spirit spoke to me and said, 'If you had money what would you do?'"

"'Take my place in the line at the ticket counter,' I said."

"'Well, are you not preaching that My promises are equal to the need? You had better take your place in the line.'"

Rees Howells stood in line as if he had the money for the ticket. "When there were only two before me," related Howells, "a man stepped out of the crowd and said, 'I'm sorry I can't wait any longer . . . I must open my shop.' He said good-bye and put thirty shillings in my hand."

This indeed was a remarkable victory, as Satan did all he could to place the obstacle of unbelief before Howells. Each time Satan came, however, Howells' faith defeated the devil's arduous attempts. Time and again God blessed Howells with added extras because of unwavering faith.

Upon arriving at the dock, to leave for Africa, these missionaries had everything for their trip except three small items. They each needed a watch, a raincoat and a fountain pen. They had not mentioned these needs to anyone. Before leaving, a friend asked, "What kind of watches have you? My son wants to supply both of you with a watch." Amazingly, his next question, "Have you prepared for the rainy seasons in Africa by getting raincoats?" When Howells replied negatively the friend wrote an address informing them to pick up two fine raincoats at his expense. Finishing writing the address, he asked, "Have you seen this kind of fountain pen?"

"No," Howells replied, and immediately each was given a new fountain pen. How accurate are the words of Paul,

". . . even God . . . calleth those things which be not as though they were" (Romans 4:17).

Can you imagine Rees Howells' joy as each need was provided through believing prayer? Indeed, Howells found the faith William Bathurst sought:

> O for a faith that will not shrink
> Though pressed by every foe,
> That will not tremble on the brink
> Of any earthly woe!

Heroes of faith

Mary Slessor was another godly saint who removed unbelief from her life. Fortified with unfailing faith she performed a lasting labor of love in West Africa. Once asked what prayer meant to her, she quietly replied, "My life is one long, daily, hourly record of answered prayer for physical health, for mental overstrain, for guidance given marvelously, for errors and dangers averted, . . . for food provided at the exact hour needed, for everything that goes to make up life and my poor services. I can testify with a full and often wonder-stricken awe that I believe God answers prayer." Then, with certain confidence she adds, "I know God answers prayer."

Are we really convinced God answers prayer? Why do many travel life's journey uttering prayers but doubting answers? Picture Joshua, an Old Testament hero of faith. He, one of twelve commissioned by Moses to survey the promised land, brought a positive report. Ten came crying, "There are giants in the land . . . we cannot seize it." Joshua, however, is one of two taking the positive approach. His simple faith grew and blossomed, accompanying a man from wilderness wandering to falling walls at Jericho. Jericho is an excellent example of how prayer and faith combined remove an otherwise impenetrable barrier. *In prayer*

Joshua received God's battle plan promising victory over Israel's enemy. *In faith* Joshua led Israel around towering walls, mentally visualizing every stone tumbling to the ground. Here is *praying faith* in action. Prayer — real prayer — sees the answer coming before it actually arrives.

Thank God for those who have left examples of believing prayer. The author of Hebrews' faith chapter lists only a few who occupy faith's hall of fame. They earned this honor not by works, but by unshackled faith in God. God's list includes men such as Enoch, Abraham, David and Samuel. All were men of prayer — *believing men of prayer*. Each earned status by total confidence in His Word. The motto of Moses could simply be stated, "Thus saith the Lord."

The kind of faith these saintly men possessed will always give Christians confidence. Read afresh God's compliment to conquerors of unbelief. . . .

"Through faith they fought whole countries and won. They did what was right and received what God had promised. They shut the mouths of lions, put out fierce fires, escaped being killed by the sword. They were weak but became strong; they were mighty in battle and defeated the armies of foreigners. Through faith women received their dead raised back to life.

"Others died under torture, refusing to accept freedom, in order to be raised to a better life. Some were mocked and whipped, and others were tied up and put in prison. They were stoned, they were sawn in two, they were killed with the sword. They went around clothed in skins of sheep or goats, poor, persecuted, and mistreated" (Hebrews 11:33-37, *Good News for Modern Man*). Then the author adds, "What a record these men have won by their faith" (v. 39).

Tragically, the Word of God also contains accounts of those failing to conquer unbelief. Agrippa weakly admitted, "almost thou persuadest me . . ." (Acts 26:28). He came near to conquering unbelief but failed. Many come close to defeating this doubting spirit and some almost succeed. Faith, however, is never "almost." Real prayer consists of bold, confident petitions and a certainty that the answer will come. Until unbelief is conquered, progress will be halted. We go no further on the Road of Prayer while unbelief obstructs the path. This obstacle must come down, piece by piece. Only then we can sing with assurance:

> Faith in God can move a mighty mountain,
>   Faith in God can calm life's troubled sea,
> Faith can make a desert like a fountain,
>   Faith will bring life's victory.

3 THE MOUNTAIN OF SIN

One sin allowed in a life wrecks our usefulness, stifles our joy, and robs prayer of its power. With these words fixed in our thinking we journey forward on the Road of Prayer. Nothing makes our journey more difficult than sin.

Tragically, too often many Christians experience unanswered prayer because little things keep them from God. These barriers constantly combine to create another formidable mountain blocking answered prayer.

Sin must be removed from our lives if we wish to be effective warriors of prayer. The psalmist said, "If I regard iniquity in my heart, the Lord will not hear me" (Psalm 66:18).

Consider the dismay we would experience if we suddenly discovered God had turned His back on us. How solemn life would be if God closed His ears to our pleas. If the psalmist is right — and certainly this is the Word of God — sin automatically shuts the ears of God. When sin exists in life the necessary step to answered prayer is confession of that sin.

Satan must be bound

Sin is quickly removed by humble prayer. Luke's account

of the Pharisee and the publican describes how swiftly sin can be removed. The Pharisee entered the temple a proud man — considering himself a supreme example of holiness. He voiced the accomplishments of a saintly life. Included in his list of spiritual genius were fasting twice in a week and strict tithing (Luke 18:12).

Next to him stood a publican, his head was bowed in reverence, his hands clasped to his breast in anguish and remorse. Humbly he cries to God, ". . . Be merciful to me a sinner" (Luke 18:13). In an instant *The Mountain of Sin* is removed and no longer blocks the Road of Prayer.

The Pharisee left God's temple proud and boastful. His sins remained. The publican departed a different person. The sins had been placed in God's sea of forgetfulness, all in a moment's time. Other obstacles standing in this pray-er's way were cast aside. First, unbelief was removed. With unbelief torn away, needed faith came easy. Soon stains of sin were cleansed completely from that sinner's heart.

When sin is removed, we can understand Christ's teachings. F. J. Huegel remarks, "Much of the Savior's ministry and teaching will remain for us an unsolved riddle if we fail to grasp the significance of this great fact of prayer warfare against the powers of darkness. No man can enter into a strong man's house and spoil his goods, except he will first bind the strong man; and then he will spoil his house, our Lord tells us. Only when Satan is bound and defeated are we assured of answered prayer."

Daily we enter a serious battle with the Evil One. If we are to spoil Satan's diabolical efforts we must begin with fervent and persistent prayers. How wise the remark, "Satan trembles when he sees the weakest saint upon his knees."

While still young I learned the value of prayer and what it does to thwart Satan's progress. Once after a time of prayer I thought of the damage one hour in prayer does to Satan. In childlike manner I composed a simple motto, "An hour in prayer gives the devil a scare." While that may be simple, emerging from a child's mind, it remains true. Satan must be frightened when he sees the knees of Christians touch the floor. Satan is bound when people pray.

Real prayer is lethal

C. S. Lewis provides insight to the thought that prayer is lethal to Satan. Comprised of fictitious letters from one demon to another, *The Screwtape Letters* tell of Screwtape, a demon in higher echelons of hellish status, writing to Nephew Wormwood, a novice demon. Many letters flow from Screwtape in attempts to keep Wormwood at his best in driving souls to hell. When Screwtape sees their Enemy (God) reaching one of Wormwood's clients, he quickly writes to correct this matter. In one corrective letter Screwtape writes on need to destroy prayer. He warns: "Interfere at any price in any fashion when people start to pray, for *real prayer is lethal* to our cause."

Some chuckle at discussions of a devil capable of rendering people helpless. Satan is often pictured a shifty little man, arrayed in red attire, with lanky, pointed tail and three-pronged pitchfork. Children are encouraged to think about Satan only in a humorous way. On any average Halloween several little "devils" are certain to appear, asking for treats.

There is, however, a real devil, a fact not to be ignored. Recently a college newspaper had an interesting article on the existence of Satan. Closing the thought-provoking article was this comment, "I see you are one who does not believe in Satan. Next time you attend a party where everyone is laughing, count the people, then count the laughs. There is one more laughing than you think." Could it be Satan spends a wealth of time laughing at man's failure to remove *The Mountain of Sin?*

There are times, however, when Satan's laughing is certainly stifled. These occur as people pray. If we could only fathom how prayers defeat Satan's army of demons! S. D. Gordon, in *Quiet Talks on Prayer,* relates, "Prayer, real prayer, intelligent prayer, it is this that routs Satan's demons, for it routs their chief. David killed the lion and bear in the secret forests before he faced the giant in the open."

Gordon provides illuminating insight into prayer's infinite impact on demonology. "This thing Jesus calls prayer," writes Gordon, "casts out demons. Would that we knew better by experience what Jesus meant by prayer. It exerts a positive influence upon the hosts of evil spirits. They fear it. They fear the man who becomes skilled in its use." Screwtape was more than correct in stating, *"Real prayer is lethal."* Real prayer ruins the pernicious plot of Satan.

The third party in prayer

Often we picture prayer as communication between finite man and his sovereign God. To some extent this is true. However, don't forget a third party involved in prayer — that old deceiver, Satan. The tenth chapter of the Book of Daniel impresses this fact upon our minds and hearts.

Daniel prayed a stirring prayer and waited for an answer. One day passed and no answer came. Five days passed and still no answer. This was most unusual, for prayer was usually answered when Daniel prayed. He might have concluded that his faith was shallow.

Fifteen days passed, and Daniel faced the supreme tests of persistent prayer. Why had the answer been delayed? What hindered his desired request? Once again day dawned — as it had for twenty days — but still no answer. Sunrise met Daniel on his knees, persisting — perhaps discouraged — but never giving up.

Then it happened. On that glorious twenty-first day an

angel of the Lord arrived with prayer's answer. Before Daniel had an opportunity to question, God's representative offered an explanation. The exhausted angel told Daniel how God's answer had been sent the first day prayer was offered. While journeying with God's answer, however, this heavenly courier met a hindering spirit from hell. They became engaged in prolonged battle, lasting more than twenty days. Had Daniel not been persistent in his prayer, the battle would have ended; his prayer unanswered. But prayer continued, day by day, and the hindering spirit was removed.

The lesson from Daniel's life is simple. Satan is a real person, possessing awesome power to fight prayer. Contrary to some modern theologians, Lucifer is not a thought of mind to be discarded as a childish myth. The devil is a real being, doing very real damage.

In truth, the number involved in prayer is three not two. Man seeks God, but in prayer's battle comes another party, one seeking to block the road to God. One author describes it, "The purpose of prayer is not to persuade or influence God, but to join with Him against the enemy. Not towards God, but with God against Satan — that is the main thing to keep in mind in prayer. The real pitch is not Godward but Satanward."

How does prayer destroy *The Mountain of Sin* along with its many temptations? Douglas Steere says, "It is in prayer that you can face temptation and recognize your peculiar weakness at the moment it threatens to overwhelm you. If we stay in prayer we are given the strength needed to refuse the temptation so that we are no longer helplessly vulnerable to it."

It is in prayer's inner chamber that we find a special power against temptation. Philip Henry prescribes, "Pray alone! Let prayer be the key of the morning and the bolt at night. The best way to fight against sin is to fight it on our knees!" Here then is prayer's basic fundamental; sin's greatest battlefield is the inner chamber; its most feared enemy is prayer.

Nothing removes sin but confession of sin. When *The Mountain of Sin* is gone, answers to prayer are sure to come with swiftest speed.

Consider the moving story of Sergeant Johnny Bartek, a close companion of Captain Rickenbacker when both were lost at sea.

"As soon as we were in the rafts at the mercy of God," relates Bartek, "we realized that we were not in any condition to expect help from Him. We spent many hours of each day confessing our sins to one another and to God . . . then we prayed, and God answered.

"It was real. We needed water," reflects Bartek, "And we got water — all we needed. Then we asked for fish and we got fish. And we got meat when we prayed. Sea gulls don't go around sitting on people's heads waiting to be caught. On that eleventh day when those planes flew by, we all cried like babies. It was then I prayed again to God and said: 'If You'll send that one plane back for us I promise I'll believe in You and tell everyone else.' That plane came back and the others flew on. It just happened? It did not. God sent that plane back."

According to Sergeant Bartek's testimony, the answers to prayer came when each confessed his sins, removing *The Mountain of Sin*. This is the crux of prayer — destroy sin and God works. When sin is gone the heavens kiss the earth as people pray. It works. Remove sin and God listens. Defeat the enemy and God responds. It has to work — God says it will.

Sin Number One

Our discussion of sin would profit little if we fail to analyze our nation's number one sin. Indeed, it is probably the number one sin in the world — often rendering prayer ineffective. The sin is criticism, with its roots of bitterness and hate.

Nothing gives Satan a free hand — destroying efforts of bended knees — more than the spirit of criticism. Of all the weapons in Satan's arsenal, this one most assuredly is the greatest. In truth, what prayer means to God, criticism means to Satan.

Travel the globe and you'll find biting criticism rearing its ugly head with alarming frequency. Churches are criticized openly, often rebuked for failing their task. Certainly, improvements are necessary, but claiming the church has failed is nonsense.

Recently my church was invaded by restless, shouting youths, arguing boisterously that we failed to preach a truthful Gospel. They claimed our preaching lacked tones of judgment needed by our congregation. Ironically, all three sermons that particular Sunday discussed God's judgment. Our pastor's sermon title read, "Has America Forgotten God?" His message vividly described God's ultimate wrath if our nation rejected Christ as Savior. That night, following three dynamic sermons on judgment, these rebel youths claimed we failed to warn people of God's impending wrath. Their screaming, defiant outburst forced cancellation of the last service.

What prompts such outbursts? Why are people so caught up in rebellion today? Indeed, this is the age of the protest sign. No person or institution in America is exempt from criticism's deadly sting. Youth complain college administrations fail to recognize current needs. Ghetto dwellers criticize outsiders for failing to help, while outsiders criticize those inside for lack of effort to excel. Governments of every nation face criticism more than ever in past history. The sad and sickening spirit of criticism abounds.

Removal of a critical spirit is not an easy matter. Saying

"I am sorry," forgiving those who harbor hateful thoughts, is a difficult task. There are times we wish our lovely Lord had never said those searching words, ". . . If thou bring thy gift to the altar, and there rememberest that thy brother hath ought against thee; Leave there thy gift before the altar, and go thy way; first be reconciled to thy brother . . ." (Matthew 5:23-24). One writer said of these words, "It knocks out about one-half of the efficiency and worth of the prayers of Christians. If the church were to really act upon this principle, her prayers could revolutionize the life of nations." Forgiving others is not an easy task. Jesus is asking much of believers here. In fact, He more than asks, He commands. Brotherhood is not optional with Christianity but a steadfast law.

Praying Hyde reports learning an important lesson concerning fault-finding. Seldom in public did critical words of a piercing nature flow from his lips. In his prayer life, however, this was not the case. Once he felt a keen burden on his heart for a native Indian pastor. Upon entering his favorite place of prayer, he developed a bitter spirit toward this pastor's mannerisms. In his mind he criticized that pastor and began praying a bitter prayer: "Oh, Father, thou knowest how cold . . ." but something stopped him in the midst of prayer.

A finger seemed to touch Hyde's lips, sealing them shut. He heard the voice of God softly say, "He that toucheth him, toucheth the apple of mine eye."

Praying Hyde at once cried out, "Forgive me, Father, in that I have been an accuser of the brethren before thee." In the anguish of his prayer, Hyde begged God to show him good things in this pastor's life and as moments passed good points saturated Hyde's mind. As each good quality came to mind Hyde stopped and praised God for this dear pastor.

Soon after Hyde's prayer, revival hit that Indian church. Clearly felt was the impact of a loving spirit. Let it never be forgotten, forgiving hearts are parents to revival. The intercourse of love gives birth to God's outpouring.

The Mountain of Sin, with its plateau of criticism, must be removed. To pray with bitterness toward fellowmen nullifies hours on our knees. The author of *The Kneeling Christian* states, "If we harbor an unforgiving spirit it is almost wasted time to pray. It would be immense gain to our spiritual life if we would resolve not to attempt to pray until we had done all in our power to make peace and harmony between ourselves and any with whom we have quarreled. Until we do this as far as lies in our power, our prayers are just wasted breath. Unkindly feelings towards another hinder God from helping us in the way He desires."

Recently a church in the community in which I live was forced to cancel a weekly service because of criticism. A local television station reported the situation, and quoted the pastor as he spoke of the downward trend in membership. "People no longer desire to come," he said, describing the rebellion of his people. "They seem to resent the message of the church." The number one sin in America had left its effect on another church; criticism had dealt another tragic blow.

Jonathan Edwards offered valuable advice, "If some Christians that have been complaining of their ministers had said and acted less before men and applied themselves with all their might to cry to God for their ministers — had, as it were, risen and stormed heaven with their humble, fervent, and incessant prayers for them — they would have been much more in the way of success."

Empty of love

People harboring critical opinions seldom change attitudes even when the leadership changes. Those signing recall-our-governor petitions will no doubt sign petitions when another is elected. I recently saw a car's bumper sticker, "Happiness is a new Governor." I laughed, thinking of its practicality. "It should be made of metal," I mused, "so they can use it when the next Governor is elected." In reality, critical people are never satisfied. A rebellious spirit hinders satisfaction, leaving men empty of love.

If we would only learn to pray for our leaders! They seem to reach out trembling hands, begging us for prayer. John Welsh begged his congregation, "Pray for your pastor. Pray for his body that he may be kept strong and spared many years. Pray for his soul, that he may be kept humbled and holy, a burning and shining light. Pray for his ministry, that it may be abundantly blessed, that he may be anointed to preach good tidings. Let there be no secret prayer without naming him before your God, no family prayer without carrying your pastor in your hearts to God."

Relatives of the critical spirit also wait for pray-ers seeking to remove *The Mountain of Sin* from their lives. The chasm of hate-filled hearts and the ridge of jealousy loom large. Sin's deceit clouds the peak of pride ahead. The summit is filled with evil places — envy, greed, malice, lust, prejudice, and lies — all used by Satan in his quest to kill the power of prayer.

Before continuing on the Road of Prayer we must destroy these obstacles. Our prayers must drive Satan back, removing his effect from our lives.

One writer observes, "The Master says, 'Faith as big as a mustard seed (you cannot measure the strength of the mustard seed by its size) will say to this mountain — Remove!' Mark keenly — the direction of the faith is towards the obstacle. Its force is against the enemy."

We must learn the greatest hindrance to effective prayer is sin, and Satan's greatest goal is to keep us from our knees. Someone said, "If there were no devil there would be no difficulty in prayer. It is the evil one's chief aim to make prayer impossible."

Though the task is rough — the mountain high — we must move on. *Impossible* must be dropped from prayer's vocabulary. We must face this obstacle on the Road of Prayer with Paul's words of confidence; "I can do all things through Christ who strengtheneth me" (Philippians 4:13).

Have you any rivers you think are uncrossable?
    Have you any mountains you can't tunnel through?
God specializes in things thought impossible,
    and He will do what no other power can do.

4   AN AVALANCHE OF EXCUSES

"So we come to one of the crying evils of these times," wrote Bounds, "maybe of all times — little or no praying. Of these two evils, perhaps little praying is worse than no praying." Bounds qualifies his statement by saying, "Little praying is a kind of make-believe, a salve for the conscience, a farce and a delusion."

There can be no finer introduction to the excuses for lack of prayer than this quotation of Bounds. Man makes countless excuses covering almost any situation. In truth, there is a sad trend of rationalization present in modern man.

Prisons are packed with inmates giving scores of excuses why they are incarcerated.

"Why did you fail the test?" a mother asks. The child's immediate reply is an excuse — a form of rationalization — "The teacher asked what we hadn't studied."

"Why were you speeding?" asks the officer. The typical reply, "Everyone is going over the limit; why shouldn't I?"

A storehouse of excuses

Satan has a storehouse of tricks that hinder the prayers of hungry Christians. Excuse-making is no exception. The devil rejoices when Christians cultivate fields of excuses.

A fable tells of a man having an unusual dream in which he descends to the council rooms of hell. There a host of demons had gathered, discussing methods of curtailing surges of revival. Satan's army had become alarmed at the number of new Christian converts. This buzz session was organized as a last-ditch effort to stop revival.

"What shall we do?" asked Satan. A daring demon stood, shouting, "I have it . . . I have the answer; I know what we can do."

"Let it out," cried Satan. "We tell people there is no heaven or hell . . . we say men die like animals, having no afterlife."

Satan's face fell as he answered, "It will never work, demon — man is not to be assumed ignorant." Then Satan adds, "Even atheists tell of times they sense a tomorrow after death."

Jubilantly another demon intoned, "Here's the solution. Let's say God is dead, and though He started the universe, He now has left it."

Satan replies in dismay: "Man is too sensible for that. Some may swallow this, but these are fools. Most believe the psalmist's words, 'The fool hath said in his heart there is no God!' No, that will never do."

Other ideas were presented, but none brought hope. Fear of failure gripped those charting plans to stop the rapid rate of revival.

Finally, when ultimate gloom faced them, Satan leaped in glee, "I have it! A sure solution!" Demons listened intently to the master plan.

"Go back and tell them God is real and the Bible is God's Word."

A gasp came from the group as Satan continued his strange command. "Tell them Jesus Christ is God's Son, freeing men from sin." Surely Satan had gone mad!

With a smirking smile Satan added, "Then, brothers, tell them the best time to choose Christ is later. Help them make excuses." Dancing in delight, the demons realized a workable plan was discovered.

Suddenly the sleeping man awoke, completely changed. He had seen the subtle scheme Satan puts in minds of men. In reality, Satan uses every means to destroy the Christian's prayer life. Forces of good and evil contend for the world. If we would, we could add immeasurable power to God's army of prayer warriors. Yet, we hold back from closets of prayer, our lips are sealed, our hands hang limply by our side, and we hinder the very cause we claim to believe in so deeply. Prayer lives suffer severely because of the multitude of excuses which are conjured up. No library could contain the list of irresponsible excuses man makes to keep from prayer. We must become surgeons — cutting out this cancer of excuses hindering prayer.

Prayer is the highest order of business, for it links a powerless human to the creative force of God's sovereign power. When people cease to pray — no matter the reasons — Christians backslide, youth rebel, preachers leave pulpits, mission fields close, and denominations die.

Prayer demands our best

Prayer demands our best. God is not pleased with a few moments at the close of a weary day when strength is at lowest ebb. He longs for us to give our best in traveling the Road of Prayer.

Charles H. Spurgeon preached, "God forbid that our prayer should be a mere leaping out of bed and kneeling down, and saying anything that comes first to mind. On the contrary, may we wait upon the Lord with holy fear and sacred awe."

God's heart must break when listening to a never-ending

tally of excuses as we rationalize away our need for prayer. A saintly man said, "One day we fail to pray because our head aches, the next because it has ached, and three more lest it should ache again."

Pray daily and watch the effect on this Satanic spirit of rationalization. Start today spending time in God's presence before embarking on routine obligations. Henry Drummond advises, "Ten minutes spent in the presence of Christ every day, aye, two minutes, will make the whole day different." Franklin Field says, "The great dividing line between success and failure can be expressed in five words: 'I did not have the time.' "

The "too busy" syndrome

Some ask, "How long need I pray?" Intercessors who have a burden for the lost and realize the worth of souls will never ask this question. To these warriors, prayer is our only hope of reaching a dying world.

"I am too busy," many cry, as souls move endlessly to hell. Our whole society thinks itself too busy to respect God who gave them all they possess. Psychologists call this the "too busy syndrome." Daniel must have had this age in mind: ". . . Many shall run to and fro, and knowledge shall be increased" (Daniel 12:4).

Consider the pace man follows in these closing decades of the twentieth century. In the sixteenth century Ferdinand Magellan took three years to make the first trip around the world. Today, a jet filled with four hundred passengers can accomplish this in less than thirty-six hours. Astronauts fly earth's circumference in less than ninety minutes. Americans have over 100 million cars, some thirty-six for every mile of paved road, another fact indicating man's rapid pace of life.

In religious circles this busyness is alarming. Many Christians are too busy to love, too busy to share, too busy to care, and too busy to pray. Due to vast involvement in secular fields, the willing pray-ers must pray much more. A wise Christian observes, "We say we are too busy to pray. But, the busier our Lord was, the more He prayed." Hildersam cried, "When thou feelest most indisposed to prayer yield not to it, but strive and endeavor to pray even when thou thinkest thou canst not pray." An unknown poet penned these words:

> When prayer delights thee least, then
>   learn to say,
> Soul, now is greatest need that thou
>   must pray.

The true Christian life is a demanding one, and those who want to live for God must take time to pray. Excuses are not fabricated by those who live close to God. Just as we obey traffic laws or pay a fine when we disobey them, so God's laws are not broken without penalty.

We must pray or pay the price. This is God's law and no excuse diminishes its validity. Godly leaders of past eras feared breaking this law. S. D. Gordon commented, "Those leaders for God have always been men of prayer above everything else. They are men of power in other ways, preachers, men of action, with power to sway others but above all else men of prayer. They give prayer first place."

Consider the disciples. When they made excuses, little was done to build God's kingdom. They had to learn that no excuse should keep them from times of prayer. Christ taught them to preface their actions with prayer. Rev. Thomas Payne, in *Prayer — The Greatest Force on Earth,* relates, "When the apostles prepared for Pentecost they continued in one accord in prayer and supplication. When they would select one to fill the place of Judas, they prayed. When they received three thousand into the church at Jerusalem, they all continued steadfastly in prayer. When Peter and John went into the temple, it was at the hour of prayer. They prayed in the prison, they prayed in the palace, and they prayed in the cottage. They prayed everywhere, lifting up holy hands without wrath and doubting."

Fear of fanaticism

An excuse that often impedes progress on the Road of Prayer involves a fear of fanaticism. Ministers are often accused of being "on a tangent" if they preach much on prayer. College students in our Bible institutes are sometimes dubbed "fanatic" if they have a regular time of prayer. But regular, fervent prayer never lowers a Christian to the level of fanaticism. The emotions of one person may be more apparent than those of another, but prayer is not to blame. True praying may compel men to weep, elevating them to where they feel God's heartbeat. This, however, is never to be construed as fanaticism. Jesus was not a fanatic but a Savior. Luke records His anguished prayer in the Garden of Gethsemane (Luke 22:44). Those who use excuses such as fear of fanaticism seem to develop an immunity toward prayer. None, however, can find the way to God without traveling the Road of Prayer.

Another common excuse involves a false humility. Jesus often spoke of the value of humility, yet He never demands that we whip ourselves for failure. God calls for hallowed and humbled spirits, yet He says, ". . . Come boldly unto the throne of grace . . ." (Hebrews 4:16).

There is yet another excuse that acts as a roadblock. Churches are filled with Christians afraid to pray in public. Many fear praying aloud because they think their ability is not sufficient to pray before a group. One author interjects,

"God does not look at the length or breadth or polish of our prayers. He looks and listens to the Spirit's voice reproduced in and through us."

Bound by excuse

Don't be fooled by the Satanic argument that claims prayer can wait. Don't become a talker about prayer instead of a doer. It has been said, "Truly great people of the earth are people who pray. This does not mean those who talk about prayer, but those who take time to pray." In truth, after all is said and done, more is said than done. Let us cast aside foolish excuses and humbly journey to inner chambers, pleading, "Teach us, Lord, to pray."

Do not think that your fears are impossible to overcome, for God has promised to make us "more than conquerors." The Bible provides numerous examples of overcoming saints. Yet, even these saints failed at times.

In Eden God asked Adam why he took the fruit. An excuse was quick in coming: "Eve did it." Eve was also confronted with her sin, but she placed blame on Satan. Though Adam and Eve made excuses, sin's penalty remained. Adam's excuse may seem partially valid, but in the last analysis a penalty was inevitable and neither excuse was accepted. Both were judged guilty.

Moses did not always stand so tall. Consider his excuses when God called him to free enslaved Israel. Excuse after excuse was presented. After the supply of excuses was exhausted Moses heeded God's call.

Recall Aaron, first high priest of Israel. Moses returned from Mt. Sinai holding God's law. He saw God's people oblivious to the sacredness of the moment, bathing in a river of idolatry, worshiping a golden calf. When confronted with the seriousness of the situation, Aaron retaliated by giving an excuse, "I put gold in the fire and this golden calf came out." This sounds as shabby as some excuses people use in missing times of prayer.

The wait for convenience

The New Testament also contains a long list of excuse-makers. Paul, chief apostle, had a challenging discussion with Governor Felix. Paul, no doubt, used education and logic, coupled with the impact of the Gospel, to drive this intellectual leader to a moment of decision. Felix sat in quiet contemplation very close to Christian commitment. Then, as always, Satan slyly advised, "Think this over, Felix — choose another day." Here it is again: the most common of excuses. Felix said, "Go thy way for this time; when I have a *convenient* season, I will call for thee."

Note the word *convenient* in the reply of Felix. Our nation waits a *convenient* time to change its downward trend toward immorality. Sinners wait for a *convenient* time to make things right with God. Christians wait for a *convenient* time to pray. People everywhere wait for convenience. God, however, calls men everywhere to make today a convenient time for prayer. If we continue ignoring God's call He may force us to take time for prayer. Robert Murray McCheyne had a special word of warning for pastors: "Give yourselves to prayer and the ministry of the Word. If you do not pray, God will probably lay you aside from your ministry, as He did me, to teach you to pray."

Time and again we are admonished to pray, yet we ignore the challenge. Days pass as Satan-sent excuses bind Christians. Convenient times never come. Crime rates rise as blame is placed on lack of law enforcement. Drug abuse soars, affecting little children and youth, while we single out poorly framed laws. Sunday school attendance drops, and blame is focused on inadequate facilities. Marriages approach disaster as counselors point to a lack of communication. Few ever suggest that the absence of prayer may be the root of our problems.

The buck stops here

Prayer could change the world, but do we pray? Communists cry, "We will change the world!" and enforce the pledge with sleepless nights and twelve-hour days. Communists who register in America give an average 38 percent of their annual income to their cause. Many youth become captivated by it, willing to give all for its propagation. One young Communist told his fiancé they could no longer see one another and broke their engagement in this following letter: "There is one thing about which I am in dead earnest and that is the Communist cause. It is my life, my business, my religion, my hobby, my sweetheart, my wife, my mistress, my bread and meat. I work at it in the daytime and dream of it at night. Its hold on me grows, not lessens, as time goes on. Therefore I cannot carry on a friendship, a love affair, or even a conversation without relating to this force which both guides and drives my life. I evaluate people, books, ideas, and actions according to how they affect and by their attitudes toward it. I have already been in jail because of my ideas and if necessary I am ready to go before a firing squad."

This young man was too busy listing areas of dedication to make excuses. Imagine a small army of Christians with such prayer-directed dedication. How many can claim Christianity their life, sweetheart, wife, mistress, bread, and meat? What hinders us from writing in our imaginations, a letter similar to that above, only addressing it to the world? Bundles of manufactured excuses are in effect an avalanche that must be removed before any progress can be made on the Road of Prayer. Excuses kill effectiveness for God and render the prayer lives of Christians helpless.

Think of the many excuses Lucifer sends our way:

> Some excuses for not praying are
> tenseness, weariness, and pain.
> Some excuses for not praying are
> tangled lives and broken homes.
> Some excuses for not praying are
> anxious fears of many sorts.
> Some excuses for not praying are
> boredom, lack of time, and pride.
> Some excuses for not praying are
> beautifully articulated.
> All excuses for not praying are
> good for nothing.

Satan must no longer victimize us with entangling excuses. We must place blame where blame is due, on lack of prayer. We dare not neglect this important duty, hoping other Christians will carry the load.

During President Truman's administration a plaque rested on his desk. When things went wrong this highest official received the blame — the "buck" could not be passed. This is why the plaque simply read, "The Buck Stops Here." A. B. Christiansen penned:

> Too busy; O forgive, dear Lord,
> that I should ever be
> Too much engrossed in worldly tasks
> to spend an hour with Thee.

5 THE PEAK OF HABIT

A habit has been defined as an act repeated so often it becomes involuntary. There is no new decision of mind each time the act is performed. Jesus prayed. He loved to pray. Often praying was His way of resting. He prayed so often it became part of His life. It was to Him like breathing — involuntary. With these thoughts in mind we travel the Road of Prayer up *The Mountain of Habit*.

Sadly lacking in lives of countless Christians are good devotional habits. Often I ask how many spend given time in daily prayer, and affirmative responses are always few.

If prayer is indeed the ultimate weapon with which to crush Satan, one must certainly develop proper prayer habits. Without training in use of prayer, God's army of warriors is fearfully inadequate as charges are sounded against the enemy.

God has many soldiers, some excelling in godliness. The generals in God's army are those with holy habits of consistent prayer. One author comments, "Men who know how to use this weapon of prayer are God's best soldiers, His mightiest leaders."

A diet of prayer

Sadly, many Christians never develop good prayer habits.

If people had eating habits similar to their prayer habits, one would be fearful of their physical conditions. Ridiculing the current diet fads, some wag suggested the following low-calorie diet: First day: "One pigeon thigh with three ounces of prune juice (gargle only)." For lunch the next day: "One doughnut hole without sugar with one glass de-hydrated water." Another day's diet includes for breakfast: "Boiled out stains of old table cloth." My favorite sugges-tion: "Prime rib of tadpole and aroma of empty custard pie plate." Also recommended: "A seven-ounce glass of steam to be consumed on alternate days to help in having something to blow off."

This diet is nonsense but, tragically, many spiritual prayer diets have as little substance. Fenelon cried, "In God's name I beseech you let prayer nourish your souls as your meals nourish your body. Let your fixed seasons of prayer keep you in God's presence through the day, and His pres-ence frequently remembered as though it be an everfresh spring of prayer."

Jesus valued prayer highly. As S. D. Gordon reminds us, it was not only Christ's habit, but His resort in every emer-gency, however slight or serious. When perplexed, He prayed. When hard pressed by work, He prayed. When hungry for fellowship, He found it in prayer. He chose His associates and received His messages upon His knees. If tempted, He prayed. If criticized, He prayed. If fatigued in body or wearied in spirit, He had recourse to His one unfailing habit of prayer. Prayer brought Him unmeasured power at the beginning and kept the flow unbroken and un-diminished. There was no emergency, no difficulty, no ne-cessity, no temptation that would not yield to His prayer.

Those who nurture proper habits in prayer testify to amazing supernatural power. Psychologist William James declared, "The man who has daily inured himself to habits of concentrated attention, energetic volition and self-denial will stand like a tower when everything rocks about him and when his softer fellow mortals are winnowed like chaff in the blast. Sow an action and you reap a habit; sow a habit and you reap a character; sow a character and you reap a destiny."

Think of what a meager hour spent in prayer every day would yield. Oscar Schisgall reflects, "If you devote but one hour a day to an engrossing project, you will give it 365 hours a year, or the equivalent of more than forty-five full working days of eight hours each. This is like adding one and one-half months of productive living to every year of life." Our torn world waits to feel the spiritual impact of such pray-ers.

The best time to pray

Those developing the habit of prayer often ask, "What is the proper time of day for prayer?" Some, claiming Christ prayed in the early morning, contend that it is the finest time to pray. In my life, prayer flows more freely in late hours. It should be noted Jesus went to prayer at night as well as early in the morning. In the last analysis, there is never a time we cannot enter God's great throne room. The point is not what time we pray; rather, it is that of developing a constant habit in this matter.

Jesus dramatically declares, ". . . Men ought always to pray, and not to faint" (Luke 18:1). Raymond T. Richey, pioneer evangelical, says, "Men ought to pray when clouds gather and rain descends in torrents; when birds have hushed their songs and flowers no longer bloom; when sorrow lays its crushing weight on the heart and all is wrong with the world. Men ought to pray when it seems God has forgotten to be gracious; when souls seem bleak and barren; when the flour bin is empty; when house rent is past due and there is no money to meet pressing bills; when the job is gone and there is no other in sight."

Richey adds, "Men ought to pray when health and hope are gone and friends are gone and money is gone and everything is gone — for God is not gone. He is ever near. He never changes."

It does not matter when we pray, but that we pray! It was not *when* our Savior prayed that set precedence but *why* and *how* He sought His Father. Some think Jesus prayed only to set a good example. One author reminds, "Our blessed Lord did not pray simply as an example to us: He never did things merely as an example. He prayed because He needed to pray."

New Testament Christians did not pray simply because praying gave pious standing in church or community. They did not develop habits of persistent prayer so throngs of people would read of their exploits centuries later. These people had no idea future Christians would study their acts and analyze their words or preach brilliant sermons on the lives they lived. Early Christians nurtured habits of prayer because no other way existed to win their holy war. They considered prayer a serious business in following Christ.

Spurgeon wrote, "Saints of the early church appear to have thought a great deal more seriously of prayer than many do nowadays. It seems to have been a mighty business with them, a long-practiced exercise, in which some of them attained great eminence and were thereby singularly blest. They reaped great harvests in the field of prayer and found the mercy seat to be a mine of untold treasures."

Perhaps these early warriors of prayer started with a little time each day for prayer, slowly cultivating keen desires for extended times. Someone mused, "We must remember that those men of prayer did not pray by time. They continued so long in prayer because they could not stop praying."

Men of God pray

Men of God are men of prayer!

Bishop Asbury related, "I propose to rise at four o'clock as often as I can and spend two hours in prayer and meditation." They say of Joseph Alleine that when four o'clock arrived he began to pray and continued until eight o'clock.

Dr. Adoniram Judson, a giant for God, spoke clearly on values of creating prayer habits, "Arrange thy affairs, if possible, so that thou canst leisurely devote two or three hours every day not merely to devotional exercises but to the very act of secret prayer and communion with God."

Sir Henry Havelock had a habit of welcoming each day with two hours of prayerful solitude. When he had to leave home at six o'clock he would rise from sleep two hours early for his prayer time. This is living on the valued *Mountain of Habitual Prayer.*

Stonewall Jackson fastened firmly in his mind the habit of prayer. He said, "I have so fixed the habit in my mind that I never raise a glass of water to my lips without asking God's blessing, never seal a letter without putting a word of prayer under the seal, never take a letter from the post without a brief sending of my thoughts heavenward, never change my classes in the lecture room without a minute's petition for the cadets who go out and for those who come in."

In my ministry I meet many fine men of God who have a daily time of meditation. This is certainly essential and yet, too often these same people push aside their need for saintly prayer. Luther taught the need for both study and prayer, "He who has prayed well has studied well."

James Gilmour, pioneer missionary to Mongolia, developed a habit in his writing of never using a blotter. Rather when he completed each page he would wait until the ink dried, spending that time in prayer. He did not elevate time of study above prayer, but made both one.

Putting study time ahead of prayer can endanger our spiritual lives. Preachers do not stand alone in this problem.

In conversation with youth we find Christian teens sorely lacking in daily prayer habits. Some go weeks or months without bending humble knees before God. Yet, where youth pray there seems to be a wave of sweet revival. Let it never be forgotten, youth can be men of God if they first are teens in prayer.

Prayer is the now life

Recently revival came to a Christian college as twelve students gathered for prayer. Soon the number grew to seven hundred at the altars. The end result was a casting aside of many hindering excuses and a fresh resolve to develop new prayer habits. Revival fires flame where hearts are praying. Sinners gloriously find Christ in churches where congregations have faithful habits of prayer.

The greatest habit we can take into our Christian life is living in the presence of Christ. This is more than prayer room experience; it is making Christianity a daily thing. This is how God's pray-ers become God's evangelists. Habits of prayer build habits of evangelism. Habits of evangelism build God's glorious Kingdom. Habits of prayer and evangelism are closely related in God's plan.

We ought to always pray and to always witness. He who effectively communicates with God will effectively communicate with people. We must live prayer and live evangelism. Someone asked George Müller if he had a habit of prayer and if he spent much time at it. His reply: "Hours every day. I live in the spirit of prayer; I pray as I walk, when I lie down and when I rise and the answers are always coming."

Answers always come if we never cease to pray. Satan knows well the power of prayer. No doubt he assigns a massive regiment of demons from the pit of hell to thwart Christians in developing proper prayer habits. There is a place, however — a place Satan does not seem to reach — where the shadow of our Lord hovers over those who pray. The psalmist found this spiritual utopia. "He that dwelleth in the *secret place* of the most High shall abide under the shadow of the Almighty" (Psalm 91:1).

Brother Lawrence knew this place where Satan becomes powerless. He wrote, "There is not in the world a kind of life more sweet and delightful than that of a continual conversation with God. Those only can comprehend it who *practice* and *experience* it." There it is plainly penned by one who found this secret place: *"Practice it and experience it."*

Now is the time for us to dwell in the secret place of the Almighty. Now is the best time to form humble habits of bended knee. Yesterday is gone, tomorrow is not here. All we have is *now*. Prayer is living the "now" life. Everything we intend to do for God must be done *now*. Prayer must be offered *now*. Revival must come *now*.

Churches must grow, Sunday schools increase, reckless youth saved, wounded hearts healed, missionaries sent, preachers trained — all must happen *now*. Habits of prayer set an atmosphere of urgency no other Christian act creates. Those with daily habits of prayer realize we must work hard and fast, accomplishing our task *now!*

Paul reminds us, "Pray without ceasing." In the original Greek, *ceasing* had a special meaning. Scholars say this rendering was used to describe a *hacking cough*. Have you had a constant, hacking cough? We do not set a schedule that indicates we should cough every fifteen minutes. We have no control over the matter. The impulse of a hacking cough is always there and at any moment we may succumb to the overwhelming need to cough.

This is what our prayer life must be. Habit must lodge so firmly in our minds no matter where we are, or with whom we come into contact, we never lose a burden for unceasing prayer. This habit of prayer separates great Christians from mediocre ones.

Wanted: chapped eyes

Songwriter Ira Stanphill talked with me on the subject of prayerful habits. He said he visited a small church where a young pastor labored to establish a work for God. Mr. Stanphill went to the meetings each night, presenting God's message in sermon and song. Less than one hundred were present each night to hear such popular compositions as "Mansion Over The Hilltop" and "Supper Time." Rev. Stanphill said of the young pastor, "One thing impressing me about that man was his unusual habit of prayer. Early each day I would hear him walk down the stairs, and soon sounds of prayer would ring throughout the house."

In this church Mr. Stanphill sang to meager crowds at first, but today thousands attend this church. Success can be accounted for only by the pastor's prayerful motto: "My church will never grow while my eyes are dry." What a splendid way of expressing the flaming burden of a broken heart! Fuel for the flame is habit, and such constant prayer keeps the fire burning.

Years ago this writer selected a motto for life in regards to prayer. I penned it in my Bible and though the ink has long since blurred, one still can read: "Wanted: Chapped Eyes." Oh, that Christians everywhere wept so much each would have chapped eyes.

One great man's prayerful habits became a literal clock to those around him. A neighbor relates: "At the same time every morning, very early, he would rise and go to prayer. When lights came on in his room we knew the time for rising had arrived. It was as positive as coming dawn. Never did he fail. One could use this man for an accurate timepiece."

A constant rule

Habits of prayer affect people close to us. John Fletcher had such beautiful prayer habits friends labeled him, "An angel of the Lord." One describes the outcome of a special prayer time in Fletcher's life, "Now all his bands were broken. His freed soul began to breathe a purer air. Sin was beneath his feet. He could triumph in the Lord. From this time he walked in the ways of God, and thinking he had not enough leisure in the day, he made it a *constant* rule to sit up two whole nights in the week for reading, prayer, and meditation."

Constant is the word to be noted. It was a *constant* rule. In all our groping for a word describing habit, this is best. Even the Webster's Unabridged does no better.

There are certain things we do to stay alive. We must breathe. We must eat foods that nourish. Clothes are donned to shelter from the elements. But another activity must be added, one we must make a *constant rule,* never to be broken. *We must pray today.*

David Livingstone could tell us what godly habits in the art of prayer can do. His habit every birthday was to write a prayer. Next to the last year of life this was his prayer, "O Divine One, I have not loved thee earnestly, deeply, sincerely enough. Grant, I pray thee, that before this year is ended I may have finished my task."

During the following year, Livingstone's faithful servants looked into the hut of Ilala and found their leader on his knees in a position of intercession. He died in prayer; his broken heart soon buried in a savage land. This godly hero, dead and gone, left prayers that live today. He learned well the lesson of developing the habit of prayer. He died on bended knees!

6 THE PLATEAU OF INTERCESSION

"Talking to men for God is a great thing," declared E. M. Bounds, "but talking to God for men is greater still." Intercession is placing emphasis on others, rather than pleading for ourselves. Becoming an intercessor is not easy. Man, by nature, is a selfish creature caring little for others. Strangely, however, this is not the spirit of those crossing *The Plateau of Intercession*. Caring for others is the watchword of those who travel this lonely road.

The climax of prayer

To begin to be an intercessor, we need special preparation. It is necessary to consider certain forms of prayer, giving deeper insight into the reasons for intercession. Understanding why intercession is prayer's highest form is pertinent. S. D. Gordon says, "Prayer is the word commonly used for all intercourse with God. But it should be kept in mind that this word covers and includes three forms of intercourse. All prayer grows up through, and ever continues, in three stages." Gordon went on to list, "(1) The first form of prayer is communion. That is simply being on good terms with God. Not request for some particular thing: not asking, but simply enjoying Him, loving Him . . . talking to Him without words. (2) The second form of prayer is petition. Petition is a definite request of God for something I need. A man's whole life is utterly dependent upon the giving hand of God. (3) The third form of prayer is intercession. True prayer never stops with petition for one's self. It reaches out for others. Intercession is the *Climax of Prayer*. The first two are necessarily for self; this third is for others."

The climax of prayer exists when people discard petty whims and think first of those less fortunate. Intercession battles poverty-gripped ghettos where people starve for lack of love and food. Intercession engages in conflict with a million evils facing our fellowmen. An intercessor must bid farewell to self and welcome the burdens of humanity. In truth, the climax of prayer is intercession.

The scope of intercession

David Wilkerson, founder of Teen Challenge International, is a modern example of one who learned well the lessons of intercession. In extended times of prayer God moved him concerning problem youth. He reflects how, during prayer, he was drawn to a national magazine with sketches of several rebellious youth from New York. They were involved in a brutal criminal act that shocked our nation. Suddenly a burden of intercessory prayer gripped Dave Wilkerson's heart and a love was born for these lost, frustrated youth.

This time of intercession was the impetus which led Rev. Wilkerson to found the greatest private organization in the world for treating hopeless drug addicts. Today his movement aids problem youth in all walks of life.

Teen Challenge, now a multi-million dollar organization, began when one man united with God in humble prayer. Today it reaches most major cities in the United States, and many cities of the world. Dave Wilkerson is indeed an example of an intercessor.

Recently I visited Teen Challenge headquarters in New York City. I shall never forget standing in that inner city center. There a former addict taught me what it means to intercede. He pointed out, "All souls won on the streets are first won in prayer!" Few people realize the power of intercessory prayer. One author notes, "Every convert is the result of the Holy Spirit's pleading in answer to the prayers of some believer."

Word reached me recently of an amazing victory of intercessory prayer in my home church. Our pastor had prayed for years for a wicked man who resisted God. The man's wife, too, became an intercessor. Daily she prayed for her husband, that he might be saved. Finally, the day arrived as her mate accepted Christ. Another victory for intercessory prayer. Intercession is basically love praying. In the very truest sense, intercession is love on its knees. When we love someone we seek his very best. Douglas V. Steere wrote, "If I really engage in prayer, 'The business of business' as Bernard of Clairvaux called it, I really awaken to the love with which I am encompassed." Later he elaborated, "When we begin to pray for another, we begin to know and to understand and to cherish him as never before. There is vivid confirmation of Phillips Brooks' well-known word that 'If you want to know the worth of a human soul, try to save one.'"

Imagine occupying God's throne and seeing one lost, lonely soul. Could we give our only son! Would we love others enough to pay this price? Sacrificial prayer is true intercession. In truth, *prayer for other men is the scope of intercession.*

"No one seemed to care"

We live in a fast-paced society with few caring for those

around them. In a large West Coast city a policeman was almost kicked to death by a pack of rebellious youths. Hundreds filed past, glancing quickly as blood flowed freely. None stopped to question. No one offered help! Rebels kept on beating, finally leaving him for dead. Blood on the pavement seemed to form five frightful words — *no one seemed to care*. Even more tragic is how Satan pushes helpless souls around while Christians lack concern. Intercession is our only means to hinder Satan's drive, yet few cultivate this kind of prayer. Oh, that God would place a burning drive within us to pray this type of prayer.

Troubled Job learned a priceless lesson about intercessory prayer. Early in his prayer experience he thought only of his horrible condition. Daily he petitioned God to remove those dreadful sores. Relief, however, didn't come when he prayed for himself, but while he prayed for friends who caused him such grief. It was when he learned the lesson of intercession that his body was restored to perfect health. Job tasted victory only after prayer for others.

Moses knew well the role of the intercessor. On one occasion his prayer reached intensified proportions while he interceded for God's children. Israel was warned to cease its constant bickering. Time and again warnings came as Jehovah cried, "I shall destroy them." But, mark one fact: Moses cared! Using every ounce of strength, he prayed, "Please, O God, forgive them." You can see hot tears flow freely down Moses' face, as he begs, "Blot my name from Your great book — kill me if You wish — but please forgive Your people."

Anyone praying this intensely has learned the meaning of intercession. How much this reminds us of that great praying Christian, Billy Bray. They say he was small in stature but a giant in things of God. Daily he went to work inside a filthy English coal mine with the prayer: "Lord, if anyone of us must be killed, or die today, let it be me; let not one of these men die, for they are not happy and I am, and if I die today I shall go to heaven."

Bray possessed an "I care" attitude throughout life. For example, once, not having received wages for some time, he had no money. He approached the Lord in prayer. He had potatoes and bacon but no bread. He went to the manager of the mine and borrowed a small sum. Walking home he met two families more destitute than himself. He gave each half his money and went home penniless. His wife felt discouraged but Billy assured her the Lord had not forgotten them. Soon twice the amount was given them. Most agree the world is lacking men such as this — men of intercessory prayer. We ought to pray for modern Billy Brays — men who think of others in their prayer, men who care.

Every Finney needs a Father Nash

Through past centuries, revivals of consequence have come through intercessory prayer. Finney's revival rocked America's Eastern states in the first half of the nineteenth century. One man, known as Father Nash, would precede Finney to cities scheduled for crusades. Three or four weeks in advance of meetings Father Nash humbly journeyed to town. No great crowds waited to welcome him and no bands played fanfares of greeting. Father Nash would quietly find a place of prayer. During the revivals countless souls were won and lives changed. Finney's name soon gained acclaim, and his sermons pierced the hearts of multitudes.

Somewhere alone, however, knelt humble Father Nash. After revival came, he quietly left town for another crusade, there to labor on bended knees. He, too, knew the meaning of intercession. Father Nash concerned himself with others, often sacrificing the finer things of life. He had no home, no church support, and often missed the taste of home-cooked meals. Nights were spent without a bed, and clothes became frayed.

What did Nash receive for this? Little in this life, perhaps, but much in the life to come. He owns stock in two and one-half million Finney converts. Few realize how many souls found Christ because of Father Nash. Time, no doubt, will show that behind every soul won for Christ was intercessory prayer. Indeed, Finney had remarkable talent to preach. Certainly he had a special touch from God. But mark this fact — *Every Finney* needs a Father Nash! Every preacher needs an intercessor.

Consider for a moment the challenge of becoming an intercessor. The needs for intercessory prayer are staggering. Frank C. Laubach says, "All the following people need to be floodlighted with prayers: the President of the United States and Congress (especially the Senate), the Prime Minister and Parliament of England, Russia's Premier and leaders, China's leaders, delegates at every peace conference, Japanese, Germans, church members and the clergy of Christians and Jews, the missionaries, motion picture leaders, radio broadcasters, all kinds of slaves and oppressed peoples, Negroes, Americans of Japanese ancestry. We must pray for illiterates, for all teachers, mothers and fathers, for understanding between capital and labor, for human brotherhood, for cooperatives, for the enlargement of people's minds to world vision, for children and youth, for wholesome literature, for victims of liquor, drugs and vices of all kinds, for educators and better education. We must pray for hatred to vanish and love to rule the world; we must pray for more prayer, for it is the world's mightiest healing force." Laubach's list seems long, but even this is incomplete. Intercessors never lack needs to occupy prayer lists. Always flowing from the intercessor's heart is prayer for someone, prayer that says, "I love you."

Aspects of intercession

All ages, nationalities, and races may kneel at *Intercession's* summit. Physician Luke from apostolic days declares, "And there was one Anna, a prophetess . . . and she was a widow of about fourscore and four years, which departed not from the temple, but served God with fastings and prayers night and day" (Luke 2:36, 37). Here was an elderly lady possessing more purpose in life's twilight hours than in her younger years. These words of Luke are of special worth, indicating that all are welcome at God's throne.

Someone has said, "We may have a wonderful gift of speech pouring itself out in a torrent of thanksgiving, petition, and praise like Paul; or we may have the quiet, deep, lover-like communion of a John. Brilliant scholars like John Wesley and humble cobblers like William Carey are alike welcome at the throne of grace. Influence at the court of heaven depends not upon birth, or brilliancy, or achievement, but upon humble and utter dependence upon the Son of the King."

True intercessors, unfortunately, seldom come along prayer's trail. Rees Howells was such a man. He learned the power of intercessory prayer while building Bible schools, orphanages, and mission churches throughout Africa. Howells' associates say he was a man of prayer. Early in his Christian life God challenged him concerning intercessory prayer. Once, when emerging from his prayer chamber, Howells gave a three-fold explanation of intercession.

"These three aspects," taught Howells, "are never found in ordinary prayer." Included, first of all, is *identification;* law number one for every intercessor. Christ remains the supreme example of this crucial law. He was numbered with transgressors. He became the great High Priest interceding on our behalf. Christ came to earth from ivory palaces, born in a humble manger. God's Son pitched His tent within our camp, making Himself a brother to all men. Temptation became a snare to Him and death the taste upon His lips. He suffered with the suffering and walked the rocky roads we mortals walk. Jesus epitomized lasting love. His lovely life defines the intercessor: *one who identifies with others*.

Secondly, Mr. Howells listed *agony* as the next law of the intercessor. "If we are to be an intercessor," felt Mr. Howells, "we must be fully like the Master."

The author of Hebrews (5:7) says our Master prayed with ". . . strong crying and tears. The apostle Paul says, ". . . the Spirit itself maketh intercession for us with groanings which cannot be uttered" (Romans 8:26).

Jesus reached deepest depths in the sea of agony; Gethsemane, no doubt, was the very ocean floor. Here is defined the agony of agonies. Here our Master's heart was broken as none have known. His life teaches intercession's key: *learn to agonize for souls*.

Howells' third law concerns *authority*. He states, "If the intercessor is to know identification and agony, he also knows authority. He moves God, this intercessor. He even causes Him to change His mind." Rees Howells claimed that when he gained a place of intercession for a need, and believed it God's will, he always had a victory.

"Who cares about North Africa"

Amazing victory for Mr. Howells followed a week of intercessory prayer during World War II. Prayer meetings were not usually held on Saturday afternoons, but on one particular Saturday the college was called to spend an afternoon in prayer, to ask God to turn the tide of the war in North Africa. This was a heavy burden.

That evening Mr. Howells and the college came through to victory. "I thought Hitler might be allowed to take Egypt," he said, "but I know now he will never take Egypt — neither Alexandria nor Cairo will fall." At the end of the meeting he declared, "I have been stirred to my depths today. I have been like a man ploughing his way through sand. But now I am on top of it, now I am gripping it; I am handling it. I can shake it."

One week later, while scanning a newspaper, Mr. Howells read how grave the condition was that Saturday when they called the extra prayer meeting. That very weekend, according to the article, Alexandria was saved. Involved in the battle was a Major Rainer, the man responsible to supply the Eighth Army with water. Later he described the incident in a book, *Pipe Line to Battle*. Rommel, the Desert Fox, was moving his men toward Alexandria with hopes of capturing the city. Between him and the city was a remnant of the British Army with only fifty tanks, a small number of field guns, and five thousand soldiers. The Germans had approximately the same number of men but held decisive advantage with their superior 88 mm guns. One thing in common with both armies was sheer exhaustion from intensifying heat, and urgent need for water.

Major Rainer relates, "The sun was almost overhead, and our men were fast reaching the end of their endurance, when the Nazis broke. Ten minutes more and it might have been us. Suddenly the Mark IV tanks lumbered back from the battle smoke. And then an incredible thing happened: eleven hundred men of the 90th Light Panzer Division, the elite of the German Africa Korps, came stumbling across the barren sand with their hands in the air. Cracked and black with coagulated blood, their swollen tongues were protruding from their mouths. Crazily they tore water bottles from the necks of our men and poured life-giving swallows between their parched lips."

Later in his account Mr. Rainer gives the reasons for this totally unexpected surrender. The Germans had gone an entire day and night without water. While the battle raged they over-ran British defenses and to their joy discovered a six-inch water line. Craving water they shot holes in the pipe and carelessly began to gulp the contents. Because of extreme thirst they consumed tremendous amounts without realizing it was sea water.

Major Rainer, the man in charge of the pipe line construction, had decided to give it one last test. Fresh water was far too valuable for testing and therefore sea water was used. "The day before, it would have been empty," wrote the Major. "Two days later," he added, "it would have been fresh water." The Nazis didn't detect the salt at once since their sense of taste had been anesthetized by the brackish water they had been used to, and by extreme thirst."

The startling point to note concerning this entire event is that intercessory prayer was responsible. Had Rees Howells not called a special time of prayer this account could well have been different.

"Who cares what happens in North Africa?" may have been the attitude of some, but others cared. Thank God for those intercessory giants. An intercessor's concern for others often shapes the destiny of nations, changing things no other power can change.

Sowing seeds of love

This is an age when people cry incessantly for social action. Popular songs contain lyrics as, "Come on, people now . . . everybody get together, try to love one another, right now." Society seeks a force to heal man's ill — to bring about a special change. From philosopher to musician the cry is, "What the world needs now is love."

Indeed, no force transmits human love more than intercessory prayer. No greater gift could man give society than bended knee. In the last analysis, when all history is written and we stand before God, we will know what really shaped this age. When we talk with God in eternity we will quickly learn everything of worth that was accomplished was connected to an intercessor's prayer.

7 THE COVE OF HOLINESS

Billy Bray was once asked how the world was getting on. His answer, "I don't know; I haven't been there for twelve years." This hero of faith lived in *Holiness Cove,* a place of spiritual beauty reached only by prayer. Few aspire to reach this abode. Those who do sacrifice all to reach the top.

The Road of Prayer must ascend to this cove if answers are expected. Those who bid farewell to earth's thrills learn what real holiness affords in making prayer more effective.

Dress up in Christ

Never has there been a greater need for holiness. Dr. Joseph Parker said, "When the church forgets to put on her beautiful garments of holiness, though it be made up of a thousand Samsons, it cannot strike one blow at the enemy. Count the church by the volume of its prayers; register the strength of the church by the purity and completeness of its consecration."

Dr. Parker adds this striking observation: "Genius is nothing, learning is nothing, organization is a sarcasm and an irony, apart from that which gives every one of them value and force — the praying heart and the trustful spirit."

Paul told the Roman church, "Put . . . on the Lord Jesus Christ . . ." (Romans 13:14). This could be paraphrased "Dress up in Christ."

When climbing to *Holiness Cove* one plainly sees a wide road in the valley below. This road is filled with frivolous throngs gayly going their willful way. Follow this road to its tragic ending. There you see the horror at its terminal point — hell.

More leave every day to join the throngs on that lower road. The great tragedy is the scarcity of sermons calling men to holiness. Burning sermons on holiness come only from praying hearts — and few preachers have a "closet" time each day. Bounds relates, "Dead men give out dead sermons, and dead sermons kill. Everything depends on the spiritual character of the preacher." Praying Jewish priests in Old Testament times had inscribed in jeweled letters on their golden frontlet, "Holiness to the Lord."

Personal integrity and character are sure foundations for a life of prayer. As a man is, so he prays. He cannot be shallow and frivolous by nature and yet pray with depth and intensity. Our prayers are worth what we are worth!

Holiness is seeing God

Results achieved by godly men have always been backed by holy living. Holiness is doing all within one's power to become like Jesus. Holiness is seeing Christ in His completeness; doing all we can to pattern our life after His example. One preacher proclaimed, "Romanism trembled when Martin Luther saw God. The great awakening sprang into being when Jonathan Edwards saw God. The world became the parish of one man when John Wesley saw God. Multitudes were saved when Whitefield saw God. Thousands of orphans were fed when George Müller saw God."

Holiness brings us close to God, whom the Bible calls a

consuming fire. In His presence we become flaming torches spreading this great fire of God. William Bramwells illustrates this thought. Of him a biographer says, "He is famous in Methodist annals for personal holiness, for his wonderful success in preaching and for the marvelous answers to his prayers. For hours at a time he would pray. He almost lived on his knees. He went over his circuits like a flame of fire. The fire was kindled by the time he spent in prayer."

Holiness is lived, not just talked about. Praying Hyde talked little about his holy living and life of prayer. There was no need for him to stand before a crowd and say, "I have spent a night in prayer." Those hearing him knew he prayed earnestly. Francis A. McGraw in writing of John Hyde relates, "I have carefully and prayerfully gone over the facts and incidents and experiences in the life of my dear friend and I am impressed that the one great characteristic of John Hyde was holiness." Hyde once challenged, "Self must not only be dead but buried out of sight, for the stench of the unburied self-life will frighten souls away from Jesus."

John Hyde accomplished much for God because of prayer, but at the root of prayer is holiness. Holiness is the soil nourishing roots of prayer. Holiness testifies emphatically that sin has been cast from our lives. Without real holiness genuine prayer cannot be uttered. One pray-er observes "All hindrance to prayer arises from ignorance of the teaching of God's Holy Word on the life of holiness He has planned for all His children, or from an unwillingness to consecrate ourselves fully to Him."

Happiness is holiness

It is true that holiness is difficult to attain. Worldly weights often hold us back. God's Word succinctly says, ". . . Let us lay aside every weight . . ." (Hebrews 12:1).

Worldly weights hinder more prayers than one realizes. We must rid ourselves of the "sin that doth so easily beset us" as Scripture states, and "run with patience the race that is set before us."

Achieving holiness is not impossible, as some suggest. Holy living is joyful and exciting. Brother Lawrence, though dead four centuries, remains a great example. His position in life was humble — washing pots and pans in a monastery. Yet an acquaintance said, "His very countenance was edifying, such a sweet calm devotion appearing in it as could not but affect the beholders. And it was observed that in the greatest hurry of business in the kitchen he still preserved his recollection and heavenly mindedness."

Holiness to Brother Lawrence was not the result of painful endeavor. He loved living close to Jesus, "I renounce, for the love of Him, everything that was not He, and I began to live as if there was none but He and I in the world."

Those striving for holiness soon learn to live within God's holy presence. It is said of Horace Bushnell, "When he buried his face in his hands and prayed, I was afraid to stretch out my hand in the darkness, lest I should touch God."

Holiness is not a lengthy list of negatives. Holiness is never whipping our spiritual selves in attempts to become humble. It is not bidding farewell to everything in life that resembles honest fun. Holiness does not mean we abolish humor and ignore all pleasure. Rather, it is simply living near the heart of God. Holiness creates an inner craving for more of God. David Brainerd blazed a trail across North America while preaching about his lovely Lord. He penned, "I long for God, and a conformity to His will, in inward holiness, ten thousand times more than for anything here below." Brainerd did not live a miserable life. He learned the holy life is a happy life and holiness begets happiness.

Society today is on a happiness "kick." Americans will consume three and one half gallons of hard liquor per person this year. Multiply this times two hundred million and we envision a vast ocean of liquor. All this is craved to provide a moment's happiness in a trying age. Recently a teen-ager came to me from a life of hopeless drug addiction. His habit drove him to jail on many occasions. He found Jesus as Savior and began his climb up to *Holiness Cove.* He described his experience, "I have a permanent high . . . a forever fix." To him holiness is not drudgery, but real living. Holiness is happiness.

Holiness is shared

Holiness is something shared. Those walking close to God affect others. Norman Grubb says of Rees Howells, "But if at the beginning the world was affecting him, by the end it was he who was affecting the world, for people sensed the presence of God with him, and said so." Some with no religious faith doffed hats when Howells passed them in the streets. One man used to say, "You mark my words: there goes a modern John the Baptist." Evidence of Howells' effect was seen when a man, not knowing Howells' name, simply asked the train ticket collector where "the man with the Holy Ghost lived." He immediately was directed to Howells.

Charles Finney led two and one-half million persons to profession of Christ as Savior. Services were marked with the unusual because Finney wore spotless garments of holiness. He testified, "I once preached for the first time in a manufacturing village. The next morning I went into a manufacturing establishment to view its operations. As I passed into the weaving department I beheld a great company of young women, some of whom, I observed, were looking at me, then at each other, in a manner that indicated a trifling spirit, and that they knew me. I, however, knew none of them. As I approached nearer to those who had recognized me, they seemed to increase in their manifestations of lightness of mind. Their levity made a peculiar impression upon me: I felt it to my very heart."

Finney further relates, "I stopped short and looked at them, I know not how, as my whole mind was absorbed with the sense of their guilt and danger. As I settled my countenance upon them I observed that one of them became very much agitated. A thread broke. She attempted to mend it; but her hands trembled in such a manner that she could not do it. I immediately observed that the sensation was spreading, and had become universal among that class of triflers."

Finney concludes, "I looked steadily at them until one after another gave up and paid no more attention to their looms. They fell on their knees, and the influence spread throughout the whole room. I had not spoken a word; and the noise of the looms would have prevented my being heard if I had. In a few minutes all work was abandoned and tears and lamentations filled the room."

The effect of a life of holiness was felt. Hundreds of factory workers were changed, their lives revolutionized. Finney had prepared himself in prayer, but prayer alone cannot bring revolution. A praying man must be a holy man. Finney was a man of prayer — and more. He was a holy man of prayer. Indeed, holiness is linked with prayer as sterling is with silver. "Prayer and holy living," wrote a godly man, "are one. They mutually act and react. Neither can survive alone." We cannot talk of praying hands unless we talk of holy hearts. The two become one in traveling prayer's trail.

Not all are comfortable when they come into contact with holy lives. Holiness often brings conviction of the highest order. Whitefield's holiness left an impact long remembered. His first sermon was delivered to a large audience in his old home church at Gloucester. Following this sermon the bishop received severe criticism and complaints. He heard reports of fifteen people going mad as Whitefield preached. Respecting Whitefield's holy life the bishop said, "I truly hope the madness will not be forgotten before next Sunday."

Holiness and the Holy Spirit

God's Holy Spirit holds a vital place in teaching holy living. Presently we witness growing hunger by all faiths to understand more fully this Third Person of the Trinity. Never have people needed the Holy Spirit as today. He is One who comes beside us, always helping attain holiness. We must make a constant effort — ever praying, always seeking — to gain the Comforter's help.

John Fletcher, of Swiss fame, became synonymous with holiness. A Methodist leader said of him, "I conceive Fletcher to be the most holy man who has been upon earth since the apostolic age." Fletcher displayed a gnawing need to have God's Spirit. Once he cried, "O for that pure baptismal flame! Pray, pray, pray for this! This shall make us all of one heart, and of one soul. Pray for gifts — for the gift of utterance; and confess your royal Master. A man without gifts is like a king in disguise; he appears as a subject only. You are kings and priests unto God! Put on, therefore, your robes, and wear on your garter, 'Holiness to the Lord.' "

To attain holiness we must be honest with ourselves. Frankly, there are times we seem to lose footing and even times we fall. It is then we praise our Lord for being near us with His Spirit. He alone can lift us from the fall. We thank Him for the words, ". . . If any man sin [slip], we have an advocate with the Father . . . (I John 2:1). An advocate is a helper; a friend who picks us up when down. Some forget that even saintly men needed an advocate with the Father.

Fletcher told Wesley how Satan often tempted him to end his life. According to Wesley his friend was so passionate by nature he often prayed whole nights to gain victory. Sometimes he stretched prostrate in agony of grief to gain victory over self. Yet, we remember Fletcher for his holiness and gentle spirit. We, too, face moments when we feel the coldness of this sinful age. Often we catch a death of a spiritual "cold" for lack of wearing garments of holiness. There are countless times Satan tries to blow us from this sheltered spot with his forceful breath of wrong desires. Then, we must move closer to our ever-present Lord.

Take time to be holy

One visit to *Holiness Cove* leaves people changed for years. Moses came from the top of Mt. Sinai where he bathed in God's great glory. His person was like a burning star — his face shining and aglow. Moses' life was changed forever. He learned real holiness is not to be associated with mountain-top experiences alone. Holy living is a daily thing, and Moses lived it everyday. His godly living gave him dynamic power when he prayed. Moses took time to be holy; he walked with God as did Enoch. His life of holiness prepared him for his times of prayer. In truth, *holy living is essential preparation for prayer*.

Oh, that each would spend time in this sheltered spot before we lose our bravery, strength, and dare desire. We must attain holiness to be effective pray-ers. With "Holiness unto the Lord" inscribed on our hearts we journey forward on the trail of prayer.

8 THE MOUNTAIN OF SELF-WILL

Dr. Roy C. DeLamotte, chaplain at Paine College, Augusta, Georgia, preached the shortest sermon with the longest title in the college's history. "What Does Christ Answer When We Ask, 'Lord, What's in Religion for Me?'" His complete sermon was, "Nothing!"

Dr. DeLamotte later explained his sermon was a corrective for people "brought up on the gimme-gimme gospel." When asked how long it had taken to prepare his message he replied, "Twenty years."

Unfortunately, it takes some Christians a lifetime to realize the importance of God's will in prayer. Too often prayers fail because we possess a "gimme-gimme" attitude. This is why praying Christians must learn to scale this towering *Mountain of Self-Will*.

A silent surrendering

In some churches of today there is the danger of taking on a form of prayer with one intention in mind — using God. Recently I noticed a book on prayer called, "How to Use God." I never read it, for the title frightened me away. F. J. Huegel said, "Prayer is not the cunning art of using God, subjecting Him to one's selfish ends in an effort to get out of Him what you want."

George MacDonald provides depth to our consideration: "It is not what God can give us, but God we want." One peasant described his prayer, "God just looks down at me and I look up at Him."

Essential to our understanding of God's will is this basic fact: God desires, above all else, devoted worship. Sören Kierkegaard labels prayer "a silent surrendering of everything to God."

No one has learned better the value of such surrender than the monk Brother Lawrence. A simple book on Lawrence's life has affected many millions. The book *The Practice of the Presence of God* contains a friend's analysis of Lawrence: "His prayer was nothing but a sense of the presence of God, his soul being at that time insensible to everything but Divine love; and that when the appointed times of prayer were past, he found no difference, because he still continued with God, praising and blessing Him with all his might, so that he passed his life in continual joy." This is a *silent surrendering* to God. Dare we hope our friends would write the same of us when we are gone?

Brother Lawrence found the will of God because His perfect will calls men everywhere to praise, worship, and adoration. Brother Lawrence wrote, "The end we ought to propose to ourselves is to become, in this life, the most perfect worshipers of God we can possibly be, as we hope to be through all eternity."

Shadow of God's presence

The more we stand in a friend's presence the more we understand his personality. In growing to know this friend we grow to know his will. Thus it is with children of God. Often we bring petitions to God voicing them with boldness at His throne. Seldom do we talk of simply waiting in His presence.

Jehovah says, "Be still, and know that I am God . . ."

(Psalm 46:10). This is the listening part of prayer.

The fondest moments of my married life are spent quietly in the presence of my wife. Earlier a dialogue existed as we pondered events of the day. Love was shared in dialogue as we voiced personal interest in one another. Later, however, love reaches a higher plane although speech ceases. There is no great dialogue, no fancy words, just a wonderful feeling of being near one you love. Love finds completeness at this stage. Nothing more is needed for romance. We are near the one we love, which after all, is fundamental love. This, then, is how we find the perfect will of God. It is learning to live within *the shadow of God's presence.*

Remember Enoch, a prime example. "And Enoch walked with God . . ." the Bible says (Genesis 5:22). What a thought-provoking epitaph! How could Enoch fail to know the will of God? He "walked with God"! When walking with God, man understands unanswered prayer. He knows why problems often plague our way. How else could Paul accept his "thorn in the flesh" (II Corinthians 12:7)? Satan buffeted him daily, but God's grace was sufficient (II Corinthians 12:9). Perhaps Paul knows today, while resting in Paradise, why God permitted his thorn. Paul, no doubt, sees value in it all, sensing the beauty of God's will.

Only when he denies himself and lives close to God does man learn His beautiful will. When one really understands God's perfect will, the effectiveness of prayer is staggering. S. D. Gordon adds this insight: "The first thing in prayer is to find God's purpose, the trend, the swing of it; the second thing, to make that purpose our prayer." Gordon continues: "Now prayer is this: finding God's purpose for our lives, and for the earth, and insisting that it shall be done here. The great thing then is to find out and insist upon God's will. And the 'how' of method in prayer is concerned with that."

The force of prayer cannot be fathomed without understanding what submission to God's will involves. God answers every sincere prayer; not a single real prayer can fail of its effect in heaven. Answers will always come, although they may not be exactly what we seek. When asked if her prayers were answered, a little girl replied, "Yes, God said No."

"You choose, God"

Recently in prayer I heard God say, "What would you like if I should give you one particular gift today?"

This question passed from my mind, but seconds later it came another way: "If I should hand you a silver platter with one item, what would you like?" In contemplation my mind wandered from desire to desire. First, vast sums of money came to mind; money to begin a special mission work overseas. Then, I thought of perfect happiness, certainly an item valued highly. Next, the fullness of God's Spirit crossed my mind — indeed a perfect gift from God, for nothing aids our ministry like a double portion of His Spirit.

Time passed as myriad thoughts paraded through my mind. Suddenly a staggering thought occurred. If I could have one gift from God — absolutely anything — I would want above all else, His will. "Give me your will for my life, O God; with this, there is nothing more."

S. D. Gordon relates a similar experience, "I sometimes thought this: what if God were to say to me: 'I want to give you something as a special love-gift; an extra because I love you: what would you like to have?' Do you know that I thought I would say, 'Dear God, you choose. I choose what you choose.'" What a beautiful way of describing God's will. Oh, that God would choose what He thinks best, no matter what the situation. Horatius Bonar prayed poetically:

Choose thou for me my friends,
   My sickness or my health;
Choose thou my cares for me,
   My poverty or wealth.

Not mine, not mine the choice
   In things of great or small.
Be thou my guide, my strength,
   My wisdom and my all.

Our lovely Lord time and again spoke of His Father's will — the "works of Him that sent me" (John 9:4). Christ was always cognizant of His Father's will, keeping in mind the Master's plan. Once His disciples uttered their request, "Lord, teach us to pray." Jesus answered with the prayer of prayers. It would do well to note that a key portion of our Master's prayer included the petition, "Thy will be done" (Luke 11:2). Our own prayers will not be effectual if we do not first pray our Master's prayer and say, "Thy will be done."

Once I visited a lady in the hospital whose new baby lay near death. One can only imagine the agony of this broken heart as tears flowed endlessly — the pain more intense than a dread disease. Finally, in sensing the sovereign will of God this grieving mother cried, "God, choose what you think best." Heaven called this little baby home that day, as a mother wept those scalding tears of love. (It calls to remembrance those wise words, "It is worth noting that the greatest pain in prayer comes from the tightness of our grip on that which holds us back.") In speaking with this lady twelve months later I saw God's purpose. Tragedy struck a close friend and she seemed the only one who understood. She stood with the family, giving comfort none other could give. Experience had taught the beauty of God's will — the real reason for these tests and trials. Her battle, waged a year before, prepared for her a balm to soothe wounded hearts. She learned the value of allowing God to choose.

Tragedy at Christmas

God always desires our greatest good. In sorrow, however, we often miss God's "why" of certain things, observing only that painful moment rather than God's total plan.

Evangelist Kathryn Kuhlman tells of God's will. Recently I came across her excellent book *God Can Do It Again.* It told of a young couple who found Christ through tragedy.

It was winter time, a matter of days before Christmas, as Joe and Dora made preparations for the holiday. Joe was a successful television repairman, father of two young boys, Mike and Steve. One morning Joe embarked on another day's work as Dora let Mike and Steve out to play on the front driveway. She knew the boys would soon return for a taste of warm cookies she was baking. Only twenty minutes passed when a terrified neighbor pounded frantically on their door. News of tragedy was soon to set a gloom upon that house for months. Her neighbor ominously cried, "Two boys fell in the pond. I think they're yours."

Joe and Dora soon found themselves standing sadly in a funeral home, the boys lying in twin caskets. Following a solemn service, burial was held in freezing wind and rain. Imagine, standing in this mother's place asking God "why?" Follow Dora as she returns home. She tries every human way to forget. Entering the kitchen she notices two little gifts Mike and Steve made at school; gifts they placed on the countertop the day they died. She silently reads, "To the best mom and dad in the world," penned in childlike manner. Follow this broken mother just one day and sense the difficulty of submitting to God's will.

Dora serves dinner now, but two empty chairs rest beside the dining room table, constant reminders of two little boys. Try to measure a mother's love — it cannot be done. The object of love is gone. The love itself remains with no release, eating at this mother's heart like a cancer. Stay with her as she enters the boys' room, only to find a rumpled pile of little boys' clothes. She pulls out drawers of a nearby chest noticing things boys collect — bottle caps, empty shotgun shells, and children's books. Consider the anxiety this father felt. He could not eat, sleep, or even dress himself for weeks. His hair began to fall, his eyes constantly bloodshot, and his body soon was covered with huge boils. Trace his steps for a day, noticing the striking parallel with Job of old. Imagine his thoughts as a school bus of joyful children passed. Kneel beside Joe as he repairs a broken television set, moving the cabinet only to discover a child's toy. Tears flow freely as he looks in retrospect. Vividly he recalls times Mike and Steve snuggled close to him showing childlike love.

"How on earth could this possibly be God's will?" It reminds me of a tragic train wreck in which a father saw his only son killed. The father, tense and terrified, ran along the wreckage yelling, "Where was God when my son was killed?" One after another he seized people, shouting again and again, "Where was God when my son was killed?" Finally he approached an elderly bearded man, upon whose aging face appeared a look of calm. "Where was God when my son was killed?" the father begged. In love and understanding came the reply, "I suppose where He was when His own Son died."

Just as cheap and easy to rejoice

It is imperative that we realize there is a reason behind all God allows. In the lives of the parents who lost two fine boys we note the husband brought thirteen relatives to Christ in the months following this tragedy. Now we see more

clearly God's will — the "why" of it. Only with this understanding can we make progress on the Road of Prayer. We
must recognize the value of accepting all that happens,
knowing well the need to have God's plan. Here we learn
the "why" of every failure, the purpose for each trial.

My mind goes back to a classic psalm, "Yea, though I walk
through the valley of the shadow of death . . ." (Psalm
23:4). We must not miss the impact of the simple word
through. The psalmist does not with frightened eyes scan
the valley. He does not center fearful thoughts on death's
shadow. In actuality, David sees *through* the valley, *past* the
shadow, looking in confidence toward the other side.

Here we understand James Whitcomb Riley's thought:

> It is no use to grumble and complain;
>   It's *just as cheap and easy to rejoice;*
> When God sorts out the weather and
>   sends rain —
> Why, rain's my choice.

Oh, that man could look *through* moments of tragedy
and see the blessedness of submitting to God's will. Here,
alone, we find full comprehension of Paul's thought, ". . .
All things work together for good . . . to them who are
called according to His purpose" (Romans 8:28).

After conquering our own self-will and submitting to
God's will, we bask in the glow of God's sweet presence.
Here, in tragedy, we hear God's voice silently say, "All is
well." Robert Louis Stevenson describes a raging storm at
sea. Passengers below were greatly alarmed as waves
dashed over the vessel. Many thought the end had come.
Finally one, against orders, crept to the deck where the
captain steered the bothered vessel. There he stood,
strapped to the wheel, doing his job without flinching. The
pilot caught sight of the terror-stricken man and quickly

gave a reassuring smile. The passenger immediately went below to comfort all by saying, "I have seen the face of the pilot, and he smiled. All is well." Here is essence of true prayer: looking into our Captain's face, realizing all is well. Robert Browning mused:

> God's in His heaven,
> All's right with the world.

Prayer, then, must be a reaching out to God, rather than a constant groping after our own trivial desires. Real prayer craves God; selfish prayer so often craves things. We recall that communication in friendship is not always begging for things. Real communication occurs when we stand by a friend, merely enjoying his company. The author of *The Kneeling Christian* said, "All that true prayer seeks is God Himself, for with Him we get all we need."

Having conquered *The Mountain of Self-Will* and submitted ourselves to God's will, we sense a special clarity of God's master plan. We know now that Christ will not allow us to be tempted above that which we are able (I Corinthians 10:13). Here we realize trials on the Road of Prayer build, teach, and strengthen Christian lives. Within God's will everything holds a special beauty, a calm serenity.

James Mudge penned this verse:

> Unfaltering trust, complete content,
> The days ensphere;
> Each meal becomes a sacrament,
> And heaven is here.

Only the pray-er who has subdued his own self-will senses the impact of John's words: "And this is the confidence that we have in him, that, if we ask any thing according to his will, he heareth us" (I John 5:14). Without stamina to stand firm in God's will we will never conquer other spiraling peaks along the Road of Prayer. We must know God's highest will, His perfect master plan.

Müller and God's will

What does God will? For one thing, He wills that all be saved. The Bible clearly states, "The Lord is not . . . willing that any should perish . . ." (II Peter 3:9). Secondly, God wills that men seek His will. We recall a time God scanned His world, observed the wickedness of men, and purposed to destroy the earth He created. "But Noah" — mark these words — "found grace in the eyes of the Lord" (Genesis 6:8), and the course of history was changed. Noah sought God's perfect will. He sought the Creator in a rebel age. Because he sought God's will, he was given the master plan to save the race of man. How true it is that God longs most for men to long for Him. Audrey Mieir sings:

> All He wants is you;
> > Nothing else will do.
> Not just a part,
> > But all of your heart,
> All He wants is you.

God's will, in truth, becomes the key to all true prayer. Man must seek, above all else, God's perfect will. He must do all within his power to ascertain God's blueprint for his life.

As extra help along the Road of Prayer, we share Müller's six-point plan to understanding God's will.

1. I seek at the beginning to get my heart into such a state that it has no will of its own in regard to a given matter.

2. Having done this, I do not leave the result to feeling

or simple impression. If I do so, I make myself liable to great delusions.

3. I seek the will of the Spirit through, or in connection with, the Word of God.

4. Next I take into account providential circumstances. These often plainly indicate God's will in connection with His Word and Spirit.

5. I ask God in prayer to reveal His will to me aright.

6. Thus, through prayer to God, the study of the Word, and reflection, I come to a deliberate judgment according to the best of my ability and knowledge.

Few men over the centuries have relied not on themselves but on God, as did George Müller. In God's will he reached highest heights in Christian service, and remains for modern missionaries a model in the art of trusting God. All because he took this simple plan and made it work.

So, here we are, "pressing for the mark" along the Road of Prayer. One more mountain is conquered as we crush our own desires and reside in God's will.

What a prize God's will is for those who submit to it daily. It must be prayer's partner, always kneeling at our side. It's sure to guide us to prayer's answer.

9 THE BRIDGE OF BALANCE

"We should plow carefully and pray carefully," Charles Spurgeon noted in challenging his congregation to a life of balance. Jesus remains the perfect example of the balanced life. Physician Luke relates how Christ increased in all essentials of life. His mind developed keenly and His body, too, was not neglected. Socially, Christ became the example of examples. He spent hours with crowds, and yet, there were many times He prayed alone. Indeed, He led the balanced life by combining the mental, physical, and social, with the spiritual.

As Jesus walked the sandy beaches and rugged, stony roads of Galilee, His life became the perfect example of the disciplined, balanced life He wished others to emulate. Later John penned these words: "He that saith he abideth in him [Christ] ought himself also so to walk, even as he [Christ] walked" (I John 2:6). Certainly our keenest desire is to follow Christ's example. The words of the following camp meeting chorus echo this thought:

> To be like Jesus, to be like Jesus,
> All I ask: to be like Him.
> All through life's journey,
> From earth to glory;
> All I ask — to be like Him.

"Ten percent Christians"

Needed today are more conquerors who set out to be balanced pray-ers. Spurgeon preached, "To be anxious in the shop and thoughtless in the closet is little less than blasphemy, for it is an insinuation that anything will do for God, but the world must have our best."

Within the framework of our worship, dangerous habits often exist, many hindering proper balance. Tithing is one example. Although it is God's law, some take advantage of the law. Since tithe of material things is 10 percent, some assume God seeks only 10 percent of man's time. This thought becomes an evil dart the enemy has thrown. Pity the army going to battle with soldiers committing only 10 percent of their energy. How tragic would the church be with only "10 percent Christians."

There is little doubt that Satan spends much time destroying balance in our giving and praying. Of these two aspects of the Christian life, prayer has received the hardest of blows. A prayerful writer reflects, "As poor as our giving is, our contributions of money exceed our offerings of prayer. Perhaps in the average congregation fifty aid in paying, where one saintly ardent soul shuts himself up with God and wrestles for deliverance of the heathen world."

Christians cannot afford to live their lives without proper spiritual development. If lives must be overbalanced, may the fault lie in too much prayer rather than works. Church historians indicate truly successful men of God not only persisted physically, but had ample prayer time. Praying hands, indeed, become God's select tools in building a mighty work for God. Someone wisely said, "We are shut up to this: only praying hands can build for God. They are God's mighty ones on earth, His master-builders." With brilliant insight S. D. Gordon penned:

"The whole circle of endeavor in winning men includes

such an infinite variety. There is speaking the truth to a number of persons, and to one at a time; the doing of needed kindly acts of helpfulness, supplying food, and the like; there is teaching; and the almost omnipotent ministry of money; the constant contact with a pure unselfish life; better writing; printers' ink in endless variety. All these are in God's plan for winning men."

Gordon fervently adds this prescription for victory, "The intensely fascinating fact to mark is this: that real victory in all service is won in secret, beforehand, by prayer, and these other indispensable things are the moving upon the works of the enemy, and claiming the victory already won."

Constant communion with God

The Bridge of Balance symbolizes exactly what it says — a place in Christianity where we value all Christ taught. God plainly teaches that prayer and work become one. Brother Lawrence bridged the gap, "The time of business does not with me differ from the time of prayer, and in the noise and clatter of my kitchen, while several persons are at the same time calling for different things, I possess God in as great tranquillity as if I were upon my knees at the blessed sacrament." Thus the key to becoming a balanced pray-er is fusing work and prayer as one. It is living in *constant communion with God*. Rev. Calixto Sanidad of the Philippine Islands reflects, "I used to farm with my hand on the plow, my eyes on the furrow, but my mind on God." He found a secret to the balanced life, that of keeping thoughts fixed firmly on our Lord. No matter where we go, how hard the task, or great the labor, we must always think of Jesus.

A crucial lesson we must learn in prayer is proper use of time in this age of wasted minutes. We live in a busy time, where a strange paradox occurs. We work hard, accomplishing little. Perhaps we pour too much time into meaningless endeavors. One writer has said, "In this restless and busy age most of us live too much in public. We spend our spiritual strength and forget to renew it. We multiply engagements and curtail our prayers. By an error of judgment, or perhaps by the subtle force of inclination, which we mistake for necessity, we work when we ought to pray, because to an active mind work is far easier than prayer." Shamefully, some Christians fail to see need for proper balance. We are compelled to remember, however, those who pray most, work best. Martin Luther, when asked his plans for tomorrow answered: "Work, work, and more work from early until late. In fact, I have so much to do that I shall spend the first three hours in prayer."

Luther knew that prayer paves the highway of accomplishment. To this end he prayed — often and hard. Through prayer and Bible study Luther learned Satan's goal in fighting warriors of prayer. Satan tries to make them think they pray too much and work too little. Martin Luther, examining his church, noted a frightful emphasis on works, but little value given faith. From this burning conviction sprang the reformation — a movement shifting balance from physical to spiritual; from works to faith. Someone aptly said, "God requires soul worship and men give Him body worship: He asks for the heart and they present Him with their lips: He demands their thoughts and minds, and they give Him banners and vestments and candles."

What God seeks most in the lives of Christians is balance; time for prayer, time for work. Often, however, God receives nothing but moldy crumbs and leftovers of tired lives, tired because energies have been drained. Christianity, however, is not a fifty-fifty, "this is mine, that's the Lord's," proposition. Christianity is a daily commitment . . . *a constant communion with God.*

Doing grows from praying

If more ministers and laymen would attempt to maintain balance between prayer, and work, the results would be staggering. E. M. Bounds vividly declared, "If the twentieth century preachers will get their texts, their thoughts, their words, their sermons in their closets, the next century will find a new heaven and new earth." No statement is more accurate. We live in an age in which some think academic genius essential to evangelism. In secular association some Christians feel status in life is the key to winning souls. They spend endless time raising themselves to lofty heights of influence, hoping to win high-class friends to Christ. When arriving at this desired place they find their goal most difficult. They quickly realize God's Spirit draws men rather than man's accomplishments. How much more could be achieved if men sought God instead of newer, more novel methods. Cure for this troubled world is not in how we sway neighbors by notches carved in shotguns of success. The cure is Christ, and men must be convinced of personal need to have this cure. Real prayer summons God's convicting Spirit, putting in man's heart a want for cure.

We must recognize that, more than any other force true and concentrated prayer challenges men to service. A praying preacher declared, "The truth is that when one understands about prayer, and puts prayer in its right place in his life, he finds a new motive power burning in his bones to be doing; and further he finds that *it is the doing that grows out of praying* that is mightiest in touching human hearts."

Wilbur Chapman stressed connection between prayer and evangelism. He emphasized, "Revivals are born in prayer. When Wesley prayed England was revived; when Knox prayed Scotland was refreshed; when the Sunday school teachers of Tannybrook prayed, eleven thousand young people were added to the church in a year. Whole nights of prayer have always been succeeded by whole days of soul winning." Here then is prescription for revival: Persistent pray-ers become worthy workers, winning multitudes of men to Christ.

A "bottled-up" society

We would neglect proper analysis of the balanced life if we failed to consider the emotions. Emotions are a vital part of prayer.

Satan observes the manner in which humans are affected by emotion. Our world operates on emotion. Billy Graham relates, "The movie stars emit emotion on our giant screens as ladies in the audience sob and restrained gentlemen unashamedly wipe a tear from their eyes. Television stars use all of their histrionic powers to move the viewers, employing highly emotional sights and sounds to evoke feelings of sympathy, contempt and passion in the hearts and minds of the audience."

Why should we assume serving God — especially in the act of prayer — does not involve our emotions? The word *emotion* is derived from the Latin word *movere,* which means "to move." Its deeper meaning reflects a strong, keen feeling for an object, truth, or person.

Dr. Leslie Weatherhead, preaching at City Temple in London, asked, "What is wrong with emotion? If Christianity is falling in love with Christ, has anyone ever fallen in love without emotion? Can we imagine somebody advising a young lover saying: 'I would not marry her if I were you, you evidently feel too deeply about it.' How could anyone come into contact with the living Christ and feel both His forgiving love and His relentless challenge without the very deepest emotion?"

Jesus certainly left an example of our need to use emotions in building balanced lives. He wept with "strong crying and tears" over the city of Jerusalem. Certainly Gethsemane is a living example of emotional outflow. The late Dean Farrar has said, "The disciples saw Him, sometimes on His knees, sometimes outstretched in prostrate supplication upon the damp earth; they heard snatches of the sound of murmured anguish in which He humanly pleaded with the divine will of His Father. They saw Him before whom the demons had fled in terror, lying on His face upon the ground. They heard that voice wailing in murmurs of broken agony which had commanded the wind and the sea, and they obeyed Him."

From college days I recall a professor's words, "The trouble with men over thirty years old is their inability to cry." Because of pent up problems we find ourselves a *bottled-up society*. Wise is he who frees his burden in scalding tears, releasing "bottled-up" anxieties. He learns that the inner chamber is the place to drive away anxious fears.

Upon retiring to our inner chambers a vision of a hell-bound world should constrain our thoughts. Only then do we join the psalmist, "Rivers of waters run down mine eyes, because they keep not thy law" (Psalm 119:136).

Try tears

Several young Salvation Army officers asked General Booth, "How can we win the lost?" Booth's return letter said only — "Try tears."

David of old made a worthy statement concerning emotions: "The sacrifices of God are a broken spirit: a broken and a contrite heart, O God, thou wilt not despise" (Psalm 51:17).

Spurgeon's pleading cry was, "Oh, for five hundred Elijahs, each one upon his Carmel, crying unto God, and we should soon have the clouds bursting into showers. Oh, for more prayer, more constant, incessant mention of the mission cause in prayer, then the blessing will be sure to come."

Today we do not have enough broken hearts in pulpits. Not only church pulpits suffer but personal pulpits too. The back fence of a housewife is a pulpit for the Gospel. Grocery counters, gas pumps, and restaurant tables all become preaching points and pulpits. The person who weeps in prayer before standing in his pulpit is indeed wise. When people weep in prayer before confronting neighbors, chances of conversions increase. All Christians — not preachers alone — must heed God's exhortation, ". . . Weep between the porch and the altar . . ." (Joel 2:17). Bounds emphasizes, "A preacher may preach in an official, entertaining, or learned way without prayer, but between this kind of preaching and sowing God's precious seed with holy hands and prayerful, weeping hearts there is an immeasurable distance." God says, "He that goeth forth and weepeth, bearing precious seed, shall doubtless come again with rejoicing, bringing his sheaves with him" (Psalm 126:6). Here is the key to effective evangelism. It is possession of a broken and weeping heart. Indeed, the greatest blow sent Satanward is made by weeping warriors of prayer.

Consider the weeping heart of Charles Finney. Once he decided to pour out his heart in prayer in the woods north of his village. So great was his pride, he kept hidden for fear someone should see him on the way to the woods and should think he was going to pray. Says Finney, "An overwhelming sense of my wickedness in being ashamed to have a human being see me on my knees before God, took such powerful possession of me, that I cried at the top of my voice, and exclaimed that I would not leave that place if all the men on earth and all the devils in hell surrounded me."

"I prayed," reports Finney, "until my mind became so full that, before I was aware of it, I was on my feet and tripping up the ascent toward the road." On reaching town he found it was noon, although he had gone into the woods at dawn. He had been so lost in prayer, time had become unimportant. Later Finney went to dinner, but found he had no appetite. He went to his office to play hymns on his bass viol but was so moved of God he could not sing without weeping. Finney said of that night, "All my feelings seemed to rise and flow out. The utterance of my heart was, 'I want to pour my whole soul out to God.' The rising of my soul was so great that I rushed into the room back of the front office, to pray. I wept aloud like a child, and made such confession as I could with my choked utterance. It seemed to me that I bathed His feet with my tears."

This weeping man sowed precious seed and two and one-half million souls found Christ. Surveys indicate 75 percent of these remained true till death.

A time to weep — a time to laugh

How can we possibly travel the Road of Prayer and never mark the value of a balanced life? How often have people said, "Prayer is fine, but I will work. Somebody has to get the job done!" Look closely at the average twentieth-century church roster. Count those at the annual church picnic, then count those at the annual day of prayer.

Psalmist David was so burdened he declared, "I am weary with my groaning; all the night make I my bed to swim; I water my couch with my tears" (Psalm 6:6). Prayer's "wanted list" seeks warriors who pray as David — those who pray with scalding tears.

Real "joy unspeakable," is found only when Christians learn the need for work and prayer. We must understand Solomon's reflection — "To every thing there is a season, and a time to every purpose under the heaven. . . . A time to weep, and a time to laugh . . ." (Ecclesiastes 3:1, 4).

Here we sense the value of a hearty laugh and recognize the priceless worth of tears. Here we pray as Dr. Bob Pierce, "Let my heart be broken with the things that break the heart of God."

> Prayer is the burden of a sigh,
>   The falling of a tear,
> The upward glancing of an eye
>   When none but God is near.

> James Montgomery

10 THE MOUNTAIN OF PERSISTENCE

"In spite of monsoon or summer heat, the Ganges never stops; so why should I?" Words of a humble praying Indian lead us to the towering *Mountain of Persistence*.

History indicates much is achieved for God by those who pray persistently. In our secular world those who persevere become leaders. Men who work with total commitment are those earning highest salaries — ones who receive better jobs. In a major magazine recently, an authority wrote on, *The Four Pricetags Of Success*. Prescribing success, the writer states, "First of all, there is painstaking preparation. Secondly, aim high." Next, he adds, "Help others to grow. Last, expect long days and sleepless nights."

John Wesley challenged people to harness the power of persevering prayer. "Bear up the hands that hang down by faith and prayer," says Wesley, "support the tottering knees. Have you any days of fasting and prayer? Storm the throne of grace and persevere therein and mercy will come down."

Age of quitters

Much of society has forgotten to persevere. We live in an age of quitters. Society constantly seeks new methods to solve "drop-out" problems of schools. America's armed forces utilize hundreds of psychiatrists in hopes of curtailing desertions. Executives of corporations flee busy cities to hippy communes where "drop-outs" congregate. Spreading of this "quitter's spirit" is felt in every corner of the globe. Few have a striving spirit like the artist Raphael. Once he was questioned, "What is your greatest painting?" He smiled, saying, "My next one." One finds Raphael always striving to do better. This is what we need in prayer, an attitude of persistence.

Satan fears this persevering power in prayer. He hates to see persistent pray-ers. As one aptly said, "The intense fact is this: Satan has the power to hold the answer back — to delay the result for a time. He has not the power to hold it back finally, if someone understands and prays with quiet, steady persistence." Indeed, Satan has power to stifle ordinary prayer, but loses this power when people persevere.

Testimony of one dear lady adds insight to our study. "For thirty-two years I have prayed that God would save my husband." Then a diamond-like tear glittered as she added, "And this week he bowed, accepting Christ as Savior." Think of it . . . thirty-two years persisting in prayer. Thirty-two years with 365 nights of intercession.

Ask this dear one if she would live those years again. Truly she would. Every time she prayed aeons of eternal flames spread before her eyes. This is why she persisted. She saw the intense horror of a single soul, lost for eternity.

George Müller wrote, "The great point is never to give up until the answer comes. I have been praying for sixty-three years and eight months for one man's conversion. He is not saved yet but he will be. How can it be otherwise . . . I am praying." The day came when Müller's friend received Christ. It did not come until Müller's casket was lowered in the ground. There, near an open grave, this friend gave his heart to God. Prayers of perseverence had won another battle. Müller's success may be summarized in four powerful words: "He did not quit."

First cousins: waiting and persistence

Charles Finney takes us back nineteen hundred years to learn about persistent prayer. "Observe," preached Finney, "those who gathered in the upper room and the work they had before them. They had a promise of power to perform it. They were admonished to wait until the promise was fulfilled. How did they wait? Not in listlessness and inactivity; . . . not by going about their business, and offering an occasional prayer that the promise might be fulfilled; but they continued in prayer, and persisted in their suit till the answer came." These pioneer Christians remembered well Isaiah's words, ". . . They that wait upon the Lord shall renew their strength . . ." (Isaiah 40:31). They learned *waiting* and *persistence* are first cousins in prayer.

Painstaking, persistent prayer has always been a special mark on every man of God. We are told Mr. Payson prayed grooves into the floor where he knelt long and often. They say, "Payson's continuing instant in prayer, be his circumstances what they might, is the most noticeable fact in his history, and points out the duty of all who would rival his eminency." Adoniram Judson spent his life in persistent prayer. He said, "I never prayed sincerely and earnestly for anything but it came at some time; no matter at how distant a day, somehow, in some shape, probably the last I would have devised, it came."

We can change the world

History is replete with testimonies showing the value of persistent prayer. Persevering prayer has changed the course of nations. Armies have stood frozen in their tracks because of prayer. Raging elements have subsided when persistent prayers were prayed. Mountains are conquered, cliffs scaled, rivers crossed and deserts cultivated when people persevere in prayer. No one — no matter what his status or academic brilliance — could make this preacher think obstacles of life crumble without prayer. We must press on, conquering *Persistence Mountain*. We cannot cancel our quest.

A story is told of an atheist who made his home in London. His wife possessed a Bible she consistently read. One day in raging anger he hurled this Book of books into a flaming fire and stormed out the door. Later he returned to watch this Bible burn. Gazing into the fire he noted one small portion unburned. Fastening trembling fingers to the page he read, "Heaven and earth shall pass away, but my word shall not pass away." Soon the infidel fell before the fire seeking God's forgiveness. The story seems to end with happiest of endings, yet, we note an interesting sequel. A sister of this wicked man had prayed for years for his conversion. In fact, the very night of his conversion she had engaged in persistent prayer. Here it is again, the power of a persevering prayer.

There is a special place of prayer on *Persistence's* summit. This type of prayer is fasting, a form of prayer used little today. Those totally lost in prayer often lose want for food. Before long they find the epitome of persevering prayer, that place of fasting.

Elder Knapp labored daily until strength left his body. This did not hinder Knapp's prayer time. Once he said, "It is really surprising what a small amount of sleep and food we can get along with, and how much we can endure, when we are filled with the Spirit. Well-oiled machinery can be run day and night for years together with but little friction." Christians well oiled by God's spirit do amazing things to make His kingdom richer. We would do well to learn God's oil flows freely in persistent prayer.

Prayer must be intense

Some think persistent praying means waiting weeks and years for answers. Although at times this is true, it is not the total picture. A person's prayer may be persistent in a quarter hour's time. Lengthy prayers may not qualify as persistent prayers. Most important is how intensely we pray. *Prayer must be intense.* When one prays with intense feelings of humility — fused with utter dependence on God — he learns the definition of persistent prayer. Persistent prayer is frantic prayer. It is prayer with depth and intensity.

A captain of a whaling vessel illustrates this thought. He tells how years ago he was hunting whales in desolate seas off Cape Horn. They were bearing directly south in face of a high velocity wind as the ship made little headway. About eleven o'clock the idea suddenly came into this captain's mind, "Why batter the ship against these waves? There are probably as many whales north as south. Suppose we run with the wind instead of against it?" In response to this sudden idea the captain quickly changed course and began sailing north. An hour later the lookout at the masthead shouted, "Boats ahead!" Soon four lifeboats, in which fourteen sailors lay, tossed about them. Days before, their ship had burned to water's edge and they had been adrift ever since, praying frantically for rescue. The lives of fourteen men were saved. They could not have survived another day.

Duration was not the key to success for these praying men. It was how they prayed. Their prayer was intense. The answer came in ten short days, but to these alone at sea days seemed months.

Here we see the basis of prevailing prayer. It is not how long we pray, or how choice our words, but our level of urgency that counts. We must not only pray, but we must pray fervently, with great urgency and intenseness. We must not only pray, but we must storm heaven's gates with unfaltering persistence. It is this type of prayer that has changed whole societies and destroyed Satanic influence over the years.

"The Miracle of Salerno"

Rees Howells talks about a miracle at Salerno. Salerno was a city of decisive value on the Italian front in World War II. In the battle for Italy, Salerno was the real danger spot. Allied troops landed here in September 1943 to seize this strategic location thus preparing for the invading forces to reach Rome. This is an eye-witness account of Howell's activities that night: "We had the first evening prayer meeting as usual in the conference hall, and gathered again at 9:45 P.M. The meeting had a solemn tone from the outset. The Director, Mr. Howells, voice trembling with the burden of his message and scarcely audible, said, 'The Lord has burdened me between the meetings with the invasion at Salerno. I believe our men are in great danger of losing their hold.'"

Howells then called the congregation of Bible students to prayer. It was not an ordinary prayer time. Prayer was intense and urgent, and in the greatest sense, true prevailing prayer. Howells relates, "The Spirit took hold of us and suddenly broke right through in the prayers, and we found ourselves praising and rejoicing, believing that God had heard and answered. We could not go on praying any longer, so we rose . . . the Spirit witnessing in all our hearts that God had wrought some miraculous intervention in Italy. The victory was so outstanding that I looked at the clock as we rose to sing. It was the stroke of 11:00 P.M."

The story continues with amazing tribute to the value of persistent prayer. Several days later one of the local newspapers displayed the headline in large print, "The Miracle of Salerno." A front line reporter gave his personal account of the battle. He was with the advanced troops in the Salerno invasion on Monday. The enemy was advancing rapidly, and increasing devastation was evident. It was obvious that unless a miracle happened the city would be lost. British troops had insufficient strength to stop the advance until the beachhead was established. Suddenly, with no reason, firing ceased and deathlike stillness settled. The reporter describes the next few moments, "We waited in breathless anticipation, but nothing happened. I looked at my watch — it was *eleven o'clock at night*. Still we waited, but still nothing happened; and nothing happened all night, but those hours made all the difference to the invasion. By morning the beachhead was established."

One easily observes the value of persistent prayer when reading of Salerno. We see God's intention when telling Jeremiah, "Then shall ye call upon me, and ye shall go and pray unto me, and I will hearken unto you. And ye shall seek me, and find me, when ye shall search for me with all your heart" (Jeremiah 29:12).

My mother prayed

Someone has said, "God's best men and women have been reared by a mother's prayers and views, and a father's solemn consecration. Blessed indeed, is the life of a man or woman, boy or girl, who has been heralded into the world not only by pain but also by prayer — their advent prefaced by the hand of a father or mother laying hold upon God."

Nine lovely children of the Scudder family in India served Christ as missionaries because a mother prayed. Mr. Scudder reflects, "Our children were literally prayed into the Kingdom by their mother." Mrs. Scudder had a custom of spending each child's birthday in prayer.

Impact of a praying mother is certainly seen in John Newton's life. Friends say he learned to pray beside his mother's knee, where prayer's influence became staggering. His mother died when John was only eight years old, but the impact of her testimony never departed. Once when lost at sea he simply prayed, "My mother's God, thou God of mercy, have mercy upon me."

From youth I recall the manner in which I awoke for school. No alarm was set to wake me. Daily at 6:00 A.M. the cry of prayer would rouse me from sleep. It was mother praying again. Looking back at my youthful years, I do not remember all the schools I attended, nor the names of my teachers. The names of most of my early friends have vanished from my memory. Many things are vague in my remembrance save one fact which is vividly clear. Mother prayed! And she prayed persistently. Her prayers were never voiced in swift and careless fashion. Many hours drifted away in tear-filled rivers while mother prayed. The result is a family of ministers. Every child grew to serve God. Each has his special ministry. A clear result of persistent prayer.

Climb this mountain at all cost. Bridge its chasms, crevices and cracks. Conquer every inch of this great pinnacle. Tap the valuable reservoir of persevering prayer. Learn to cry as Jacob in his battle with an angel. "I will not let thee go, except thou bless me." Sing along with Charles Gabriel:

> I want to scale the utmost heights
> And catch a gleam of glory bright;
> But still I'll pray till heaven I've found,
> Lord, lead me on to higher ground.

11 BURDEN'S OUTLOOK

It has been reported that at present rates of Scripture distribution it will take thirteen years to reach all the people of North America with the Gospel. Consider further that it will require sixteen years to reach Latin America, thirty years to reach Australia, seventy-five years to reach Africa, ninety years to reach Europe, ninety years to reach East Asia and three hundred seventy years to reach West Asia. How can we reach people with the Gospel when statistics indicate seven out of eight Christians in the world do not possess a Bible?

Can we read these reports and fail to have a burden for the lost? Can we keep ourselves from falling prostrate — overcome by the agonizing burden — crying out as John Knox did, "O God, give me Scotland or I die"? Can we help but pray as Whitefield, "O Lord, give me souls or take my soul"?

World population increases even as more than one hundred thousand die each day. Man's only way to save this world is by prayer — prayer which carries this agonizing burden to the Lord. One wise writer said, "I question if any believer can have the burden of souls upon him — a passion for souls — and not agonize in prayer." Never has there been a greater need for burdened hearts. If we cease our prayers for miracles to reach this world for Christ it will not happen. Mere machinery cannot do the task. Great computers of this age are of little help. We have printing presses, television, and radio to aid in spreading the Gospel, yet we seem to fail. What, then, is the crying need? We must catch a fresh and desperate burden for lost men — a burden expressed only in prayer.

When prayer becomes desperate

We must advance to desperation in prayer to meet the desperate challenge of this age. Huegel writes, "There are times when the Christian's praying is something so desperate, so awful, so tremendous that one trembles before the very record of it." How true this is! Often we walk into prayer rooms where people tremble in God's presence. They tremble because a burden aches deep inside their breasts. They seem to bow at the foot of Calvary watching their Savior's blood drip upon Golgotha's ground. We gain a special sense of where the writer was who wrote, "Were you there when they crucified my Lord? Were you there when they crucified my Lord? Sometimes it causes me to tremble, tremble, tremble. Were you there when they crucified my Lord?"

We must climb to *Burden's Outlook* if we are to make progress on the Road of Prayer. This lofty height must be explored thoroughly and better understood. We can not cast it aside or go around.

Learn from Sir Thomas Broune, a great English physician, who developed a curious prayer burden. Once he vowed, "To pray in all places where quietness inviteth; in any house, highway or street; and to know no street in this city that may not witness that I have not forgotten God and my Savior in it; and that no town or parish where I have been may not say the like. To take occasion of praying upon the sight of any church which I see as I ride about."

Broune further pledges, "To pray daily, and particularly, for my sick patients, and for all sick people, under whose care so ever. And at the entrance into the house of the sick to say, 'May peace and the mercy of God be upon this house.' After a sermon to make a prayer and desire a blessing and to pray for the minister."

Keep the fire

A burden for souls must not be kept for bended knee alone. We must not save it just for quiet times amid prayer's inner chamber. The intercessor's burning heart must keep its flame, notwithstanding those around or the time of day. A renowned evangelist provides good example. He recently returned from several crusades overseas. While in Brazil he and a missionary attended a soccer game. They viewed the contest in one of the world's largest stadiums. Crowds surpassing two hundred thousand often gather there for contests. These men were caught amidst the thrill of this vast multitude. "This is time for pleasure" — some would say — "forget your calling momentarily. Blot from your mind the burden of your heart." When you have a flaming burden, however, forgetting souls is not easy. Soon this evangelist's eager eyes wandered through the crowd. He noticed, too, the missionary had lost interest in the game. Looking at him he asked, "Are you thinking what I'm thinking?" and heard a quick reply, "I'm sure I am." Their thoughts were centered on the mammoth soccer stadium. Could it be filled with hungry hearts in search of Christ?

Recent reports indicate this colossal stadium is available for future crusades. Preliminary rallies are drawing over fifty thousand. Soon, crowds four times as large will attend. All because a moment's joy was forgotten, and the flame of burden kindled.

John Wilkerson composed a simple chorus with this line, "Lord, give me a vision — a sanctified vision — keep the fire on the altar of my heart." Three words of this chorus ought to be life's motto. *Keep the fire!* What a glorious theme to take along prayer's journey. "Let me burn out for God," said Henry Martin. "After all, whatever God may appoint, prayer is the great thing. Oh, that I may be a man of prayer."

Hyde and his burden

Some think burdens are to be reserved for special times. For Brother Lawrence, however, the burden of his praying heart never died — the flame never quenched. He wrote, "I made this my business as much all the day long as at the appointed time of prayer; for at all times, every hour, every minute, even in the height of my business, I drove away from my mind everything that was capable of interrupting my thoughts of God."

Think of Praying Hyde who often went into the hills to visit friends and pray. A friend relates, "It was evident to all he was bowed down with sore travail of soul. He missed many meals and when I went to his room I would find him lying as in great agony, or walking up and down as if an inward fire were burning in his bones." It was from intense burden that Hyde asked God to give him a soul a day that year. Praying Hyde departed from his friends no ordinary man. He became a burden-bearer for mankind. At year's end four hundred souls had been won to Christ. As the new year came John Hyde approached God's throne with greater burden. Now Hyde begged for two souls daily. Twelve months later more had been won than Hyde anticipated. In fact, some eight hundred souls were claimed that year. This, however, did not satisfy Praying Hyde. Soon we hear him pleading, "Give me four souls every day."

Hyde's intent was not to win these with tent crusades or massive rallies. He went for every soul, one at a time. It is said Hyde approached sinners on the street of any village at any time. Conversation ensued and before long both would kneel in prayer. Hyde would lead this new convert to water and perform baptismal rites. This event repeated itself four times daily because Hyde's burden reached out to lost men. Multitudes of souls found Christ when this humble man assumed a burden for the lost.

A trip to Gethsemane

St. Francis of Assisi had a personal retreat, Mount Averno, where he spent hours in anguish of a burdened heart. Those close to Francis say he prayed for hours, never voicing any word but "God." We often look at mortals like this and quickly label them saints. Artists often place halos above their heads in paintings. Consider the One who led the way along the path of prayer as it climaxed in Gethsemane. Luke paints a picture of Gethsemane as it ought to be — not one of Christ calmly kneeling, halo fixed above his head. Luke reflects in retrospect, "And being in an agony he prayed more earnestly: and his sweat was as it were great drops of blood falling down to the ground" (Luke 22:44). A Bible commentator remarks, "Doubtless, the battle of the cross was first fought and won in Gethsemane. It is considered that the soul anguish which he suffered on that occasion was equal to that which he suffered on the cross of calvary." In reality, Christ died in Gethsemane before He ever died on the cross. He, no doubt, was nailed to Gethsemane's ground by burden before nails of Roman soldiers hanged Him to the cross. Have you been to Gethsemane? Consider the words of William Gaither:

> Have you had a Gethsemane?
> Have you prayed in despair?
> In the dark of the dreary hour,
> Did the Lord meet you there?

Burden's brother

God's word states, "Where there is no vision people perish" (Proverbs 29:18). Vision is brother to the force we call burden. We could almost paraphrase the words of Proverbs: "Where there is no burden people perish." What is vision? Jonathan Swift relates, "Vision is the art of seeing things invisible." *Vision is seeing a need* in our mind before it arises in the physical. *Burden is feeling a need* in our heart before it happens. Vision, or burden, prompts us to pray for those suffering across rolling oceans of despair. We may not suffer trials they experience, yet, we sense how they feel. We may not stand beside them physically, yet vision takes us there. We pray as they pray. We feel as they feel. Vision is ability to see remote villages waiting for the Gospel. Human limitation builds a wall of separation but prayerful vision removes all barriers. We pray for converts overseas and with vision see results. Indeed, "Vision is the art of seeing things invisible." As Charles Allen stresses, "The only limit to your prayer, says Christ, is the limit of your own belief. What is belief? It is *mental visualization*. It is seeing in your mind what you want accomplished in your life."

Out of this vision for a dying world grows the greatest vision, the vision of visions. It is a yearning for prayer warriors. This was Christ's vision. He states, ". . . The harvest is truly plenteous, but the labourers are few; Pray ye therefore the Lord of the harvest, that he will send forth labourers into his harvest" (Matthew 9:37, 38). Jesus wants all to hear His glorious Gospel but realizes workers are few. Christ does not say here, "Build new Sunday schools, train new workers." He does not say, "Enlarge Bible schools." No, indeed, Christ first points men to prayer. Not that we should cease other labors, but, with them, pray.

Picture Dr. Bacchus of Hamilton College as he lay near death. His doctor entered the room and quietly gave him a quick examination. With a solemn look he departed. Passing through the door he softly spoke to friends standing by.

"What did the doctor say?" asked Mr. Bacchus.

"He said, Sir, you cannot live more than half an hour."

"Then take me out of bed," cried Bacchus, "and place me on my knees. Let me spend the time in prayer for this sinful world." Moments later Dr. Bacchus passed from bended knees to Paradise.

What a beautiful vision Dr. Bacchus possessed! Few will ever realize how much his final prayer accomplished. No one knows how much is achieved by the powerful combination of a visionary's vision and a pray-er's burden. As one so aptly stated, "Who can tell how many towns and cities have been saved in answer to prevailing prayers of God's people since the time that Abraham interceded in behalf of Sodom."

Go back over history's records and observe the many times destinies of nations were changed because of prayerful vision. "Nobody but God knows," cried a wise preacher, "how often prayers have changed the course of history." God and Satan know well the value of a visionary's prayers. No wonder Satan condemns this saintly act God encourages.

Prayer is limitless

Consider John Wesley's burden. Burning in his heart was

vision for a worldwide visitation. He sought revival to shake the world. Long before revival fires flamed he had a vision of the flames. In his journal he describes the start of this revival, "Monday, January 1, 1739, Mr. Hall, Kinchin, Ingham, Whitefield, Hutchins, and my brother Charles were present in Fetterslane, with about sixty of our brethren. About three in the morning, as we were continuing instant in prayer, the power of God came mightily upon us, insomuch that many cried out for exceeding joy, and many fell to the ground."

Wesley received a powerful outpouring of God's Spirit at this meeting. Soon his preaching changed whole cities. His unction and power were far greater than before. Methodist societies witnessed amazing upsurges in attendance as vision from months of prayer had become reality. Soon the world became Wesley's parish. Cities burned with revival, just as Wesley had anticipated in prayer. Richard Watson Gilder said of Wesley:

> In those clear, piercing, piteous eyes
>   behold
> The very soul that over England
>   flamed!
> Deep, pure, intense; consuming shame
>   and ill;
> Convicting men of sin; making faith live;
>   and, this the mightiest miracle of all,
> Creating God again in human hearts.

Intense prayer took Wesley's vision around the world. Indeed, *prayer is limitless*. No limitations hinder those who pray. "Ask of me," cries God, "and I shall give thee the heathen for thine inheritance, and the uttermost parts of the earth for thy possession" (Psalm 2:8). Imagine the all-comprehending possibilities prayer provides under such promises of God! The only real limitation of our prayers is our inability to ask.

God seeks men of burden

How broken God must be when looking daily for students in His school of prayer and seeing countless absentees. How it must have pierced His heart to say, "And I sought for a man among them, that should make up the hedge, and stand in the gap before me . . . but I found none" (Ezekiel 22:30). Can this possibly be? The God of the universe unable to find a candidate to hedge the gap? We wonder if the time will come when God will cry again, "I sought for a man but found none!" Praise God He sent Christ to hedge the greatest gap, the gulf of sin. Thank God, too, for those burdened prayer warriors whose petitions bridge the gap between God and man. We rejoice for men like Elder Knapp who testified, "I often repaired to the barn in the silent hours of the night, and poured out my soul in prayer to God." Every time an Elder Knapp performs an act like this, he fills the gap, making up prayer's hedge.

I recall one dear lady who stood in a prayer room on a quiet Sunday afternoon. There was no scheduled time of prayer, as she stood alone before God's throne. Our whole congregation should have been there to observe. Opening the prayer room door I could see this dear saint, her back to me, weeping before a large missionary list. Here was a praying saint, well past eighty years, standing in the gap.

Days later another incident reminded me of those who fill such a need. I returned for something I had left in our youth chapel days before. Entering the darkened room, I saw the shadow of a lonely figure on the wall. There a burdened girl knelt, crying to God. It was afternoon when most youth involve themselves in school activities. There she was . . . making up prayer's hedge, pleading that God would send revival.

How earnestly God seeks young lives to stand in the gap — to travel the Road of Prayer. Frankly, the trail is rough, the task rugged. It offers challenge not found elsewhere.

12 TRAIL'S END:
THE MOUNTAIN OF GOD'S POWER

Dr. Courtland, twentieth century scientific genius, says, "Prayer is the mightiest force in the universe." Here is a scientist's explanation of the power awaiting praying Christians. Charles Spurgeon adds, "The power of prayer can never be overrated. They who cannot serve God by preaching need not regret. If a man can but pray, he can do anything. He who knows how to overcome with God in prayer has Heaven and earth at his disposal."

The Road of Prayer has been a challenging journey. Many obstacles have been overcome on this rugged road. In prayer we have removed *Sin's Mountain,* leveled *The Peak of Unbelief* and cast aside an *Avalanche of Excuses.* Together we scaled *The Peak of Habit,* crossed *The Plateau of Intercession,* and spent some time in *Holiness Cove.* There have been other barriers on the Road of Prayer. We will long remember *The Bridge of Balance, The Mountains of Self-Will* and *Persistence,* along with the rugged trail to *Burden's Outlook.* Now before us, at the edge of prayer's horizon, towers a mountain above the others. Here rises life's mountain of mountains for pray-ers. It is *The Mountain of God's Power* with a towering peak that reaches out to God. Here we learn as Bounds suggests, "prayer can do anything God can do."

While preaching on the mighty power of prayer, Spurgeon cried, "The very act of prayer is a blessing. To pray is, as it were, to bathe oneself in a cool stream, and so to escape from the heat of earth's summer sun. To pray is to mount on eagle's wings above the clouds and soar to heaven where God dwells. To pray is to enter the treasure house of God and to enrich oneself out of an inexhaustible storehouse. To pray is to grasp heaven in one's arms; to embrace the deity within one's soul and to feel one's body made a temple of the Holy Ghost."

A sovereign remedy

Prayer is the only cure for spiritual sickness. "Enough people praying," someone penned, "will release into the human blood stream the mightiest medicine in the universe, for we shall be the channels through whom God can exert His infinite power."

Imagine a world with sickness abolished. Think how much greener rolling hills would be — how lovelier the rose would seem — if sin were driven from the earth. Dr. Payne declared, "Prayer hath brought health to the sick, hearing to the deaf, speech to the dumb, and eyes to the blind; life to the dead, salvation to the lost. And hath even driven Satan from the hearts of many, and brought the God of Heaven to dwell in his room."

The power of prayer is not merely good medicine but the only medicine for a troubled age. Prayer is the only cure Robert Hall declared, "The prayer of faith is the only power in the universe to which the great Jehovah yields. Prayer is *the sovereign remedy*." Faith-filled prayer, indeed, is mankind's key to unlock God's eternal power.

Nothing should restrain us from drawing on this great

source of power. We must ask, as Hudson Taylor did, "Should we not do well to suspend our present operations and give ourselves to humiliation and prayers for nothing less than to be filled with the Spirit, and made channels through which He shall work with resistless power? Souls are perishing now for lack of this power. . . . God is blessing now some who are seeking this blessing from Him in faith." How accurate are Taylor's timely words! Billions of lost souls seek a redeemer, while Christians seek new means to reach these dying men.

Shall we build better machines? Can computerized programming provide necessary power? Frankly, what we need is a God-given power to reach this rebel world. What is this power? James Cowden Wallace answers:

> That power is prayer, which soars on high
> Through Jesus to the throne,
> And moves the hand which moves the world
> To bring salvation down.

Quest for power

Man seeks power in many ways. His quest reaches out into God's universe as he travels to the moon and dreams of planetary exploration. Real power, however, is found only in prayer. Isaac Newton, the brilliant scientist, relates, "I can take my telescope and look millions of miles into space but I can lay my telescope aside, get down on my knees in earnest prayer and I see more of heaven and get closer to God than I can when assisted by all the telescopes and material agencies on earth."

The power of prayer reaches every human need. Prayer provides the power for saving souls, for the cure of diseases, for victory in battles, for sleepless nights and trials. Prayer grants power for conflicts of old age, for calmness in the tempest, for comfort during sorrow, and guidance in life's storms. Our list grows as we consider the possibilities of prayer. Man in quest of real power finds it in faith-filled prayer. Jesus says, ". . . ask any thing in my name, I will do it" (John 14:14). One word sums up what prayer can do. Anything!

Church achievements are directly related to its prayer life. Churches ignoring prayer refuse the only real world-changing power. Rev. Mark Guy Pearce declares, "The prayer meeting is the thermometer of the church. It tests what degree of warmth there is. The prayer meeting is the barometer of the church and points to showers of blessing or seasons of drought. The church's warming apparatus is the prayer meeting room." Unfortunately, many churches no longer place enough value on prayer. Congregations often fail to recognize prayer as man's best weapon. Bounds, challenging preachers, cried, "The preaching man is to be the praying man. Prayer is the preacher's mightiest weapon." Prayer is everyone's best weapon, not the preacher's alone. We are reminded of America's powerful howitzer cannons of World War II. Without ammunition, however, these guns could not be considered weapons of war. This is why our enemies sought first to destroy our munition dumps. Likewise, Christians are rendered useless without prayer. Satan's goal becomes clear. He desires to destroy the Christian's ammunition storehouse, the secret place of prayer.

Prayers are deathless

"Prayer is not given us as a burden to be borne," wrote a man of God, ". . . but to be a joy and a power to which there is no limit." The greatness and power of prayer provide Christians the greatest challenge. It is not a gruesome task or irksome duty. The art of the bended knee is a royal honor of the highest order. Prayer is man's highest privilege, his greatest responsibility. It places in our human hand God's sovereign power. Prayer, genuine prayer, is the most powerful act a creature of God can perform.

The power gained on bended knee has accomplished more for God than all combined forces of Christianity in two millenia. Works are fine, but works die with men. A remnant of man's works may live but to a great extent they die. Prayer, however, lives. Prayer is power uncontained by death or grave. A praying man relates, "God changes the world by prayer, *prayers are deathless,* the lips that uttered them may be closed in death, the heart that felt them may have ceased to beat, but prayers . . . outlive the lives of those who uttered them; outlive a generation, outlive an age, outlive a world." The power of prayer is not reserved for any certain class of people. Historians tell us Whitefield took a little crippled man with him to crusades. His job was not crusade director nor chief musician. He prayed! That was the extent of his duty. As Whitefield preached, this handicapped Christian prayed. Now we see more clearly why Whitefield's sermons rocked the hearts of men.

The vividness with which he preached seemed supernatural. Once, while preaching to sailors, he described a vessel lost at sea. He portrayed her as on her side, ready to sink, and then cried aloud, "What next?" So anointed was Whitefield's preaching that sailors sprang to their feet, crying, 'The life boat! Grab the life boat!" On another occasion he pictured a blind man walking near the edge of a precipice. Without knowing where he was going he came to the edge. Whitefield's portrayal was so vivid at this point that the famous Lord Chesterfield sprang to his feet crying, "My God! He's gone!" Famous actors Garrick, Foote, and Shuter loved to hear Whitefield preach. Garrick was so impressed he declared Whitefield could make people weep by the mere enunciation of the word, "Mesopotamia." So run the accounts of Whitefield's anointed preaching. Yet, remember a little crippled man's prayers. Early morning and late night we see those twisted legs bending in supplicating prayer.

Potency of prayer

Writers attempt to adequately describe the essence of prayer. Authors amass words, expressions, and clichés to explain it. Volumes have been penned to stress it. Yet, a simple word describes it — *power!* "Prayer brings power," writes Gordon. "Prayer is power, the time of prayer is the time of power. The place of prayer is the place of power. Prayer is tightening the connections with the divine dynamo so power may flow freely without loss or interruption." This defines true prayer. It is power to defeat Satan's hellish demons any place, any time, no matter what odds. "More things are wrought by prayer than this world dreams of," cries Tennyson. In fact, more dread blows are driven Satanward by prayer than hell would care to mention.

Before his death, Dale Carnegie was kind enough to share this secret of his life. "Every day I pray. I yield myself to God, and tensions and anxieties go out of me and peace and power come in." True prayer — coming from those in the right standing with Christ — brings untold blessings and power. By means mortals cannot comprehend, prayer releases inward tension and anxieties. A noted psychiatrist reports, "After a long life observing human behavior, I have no doubt, whatever, that entirely apart from its religious significance, prayer is one of the most effective methods of tapping the wisdom and power that exists in the great reservoir of the unconscious." People reflect inward peace following prayer. Recently scores of Christian teenagers gathered for a weekend devoted only to prayer. Being present, I decided to watch closely the results. Most noticeable was a special happiness each teen possessed following the prayer camp. Anxious, troubled teens departed free from cares — a fact demonstrating the power of prayer over life's attitudes. Prayer, indeed, touches every aspect of human experience. Prayer is power, for it links man to God's sovereign power source, His Holy Spirit. ". . . Ye shall receive power, after that the Holy Ghost is come upon you . . ." (Acts 1:8). Luke said it, Pentecost proves it, and God still chooses to extend this power to praying men. Chrysostom said it dramatically:

"The potency of prayer hath subdued the strength of fire; it hath bridled the rage of lions, hushed anarchy to rest, extinguished wars, appeased the elements, expelled demons, burst the chains of death, expanded the gates of heaven, assuaged diseases, repelled frauds, rescued cities from destruction, stayed the sun in its course and arrested the progress of the thunderbolt. Prayer is an all-efficient panoply, a treasure undiminished, a mine which is never exhausted, a sky unobscured by clouds, a heaven unruffled by the storm. It is the root, the fountain, the mother of a thousand blessings."

Heroes of the closet

We cannot leave this discussion of the power of prayer without recalling heroes of the faith from former years. Perhaps we should label them *heroes of the closet,* for here they gained needed faith for service. Truly, heroes of the closet are heroes of the faith. Look again at Praying Hyde. Hyde's prayer power stimulated thousands for Christ. Dr. J. Wilbur Chapman recalls the time he spent praying with Hyde:

"He came to my room, turned the key in the door, dropped on his knees, and waited five minutes without a single syllable coming from his lips. I knew I was with God. Then with upturned face, down which the tears were streaming he said, 'O God.'"

Recalling this joyous time Chapman adds, "Then for five

minutes at least, Hyde was still again, and then when he knew he was talking with God his arms went around my shoulder and there came up from the depth of his heart such petitions for men as I had never heard before. I rose from my knees to know what real prayer was." Such results are gained only when people touch God through unwavering prayer.

Elder Jacob Knapp was another hero of the closet. Knapp was so endued with prayer's power his very name became synonymous with spiritual power. Reports indicate over one hundred thousand found Christ under his ministry.

Edward Payson provides another excellent example of the power of prayer. He was the most illustrious of Congregational preachers of New England. "His pulpit utterances," wrote McClintock and Strong, "were of the most startling and uncompromising character. It may be truly said of Edward Payson he labored not to please men, but God; and his pulpit thundered like another Sinai. . . ." Payson's fire was kindled by traveling the Road of Prayer.

Peter Cartwright, too, was a hero of the closet. When he preached, God's power fell in torrents like driving rain. Following a campaign, he relates, "The encampment was lighted up, the trumpet blown, I rose in the stand, and required every soul to leave the tents and come into the congregation. There was a general rush to the stand. I requested the brethren, if ever they prayed in all their lives, to pray now."

In certain confidence Cartwright continues, "My voice was strong and clear, and my preaching was more of exhortation and encouragement than anything else. My text was, 'The gates of hell shall not prevail.' In about thirty minutes the power of God fell on the congregation in such a manner as is seldom seen: The people fell in every direction, right and left, and front and rear. It was supposed that not less than three hundred fell like dead men in mighty battle."

Charles Finney, too, must have felt similar impact as a result of time spent in prayer. In Finney's meetings God's power was so intense that entire audiences fell prostrate on hardwood floors. At times God's power would come on Finney as a literal cloud. Historians say a holy calm, noticed even by sinners, settled on cities where this modern John the Baptist preached. Amazing results always accompanied Finney's preaching. Two and one-half million Finney converts stand as living testimony to prayer's power. Oh, that God would teach us to pray. Only then will we sense the positive power of prayer.

Prayer's sustaining power

Prayer's power is not given only for man's urgent and serious needs; this power must be secured for even daily trivialities. Dr. Alexis Carrel, Nobel Prize winner, says, "As a physician, I have seen men; after all other therapy failed, lifted out of disease and melancholy by the serene effort of prayer. It is the power in the world that seems to overcome the so-called 'laws of nature.' The occasions on which prayer has dramatically done this have been termed 'miracles.' But a constant, quieter miracle takes place hourly in hearts of men and women who have discovered that prayer supplies them with a steady flow of sustaining power in their daily lives" (*Voyage to Lourdes,* Harper: 1950).

Christ drew daily from the sustaining power of prayer. At dawn we find Him praying. As evening shadows lengthen Jesus prayed. Often during daylight hours Jesus stopped for heavenly conversation. Before facing Calvary He spent a painful night in prayer. Decades of His human life were given much to prayer. Jesus walked on water, healed the sick, calmed the raging tempest and raised the dead. But most of all He prayed. His private prayers produced His public miracles. Everything in Jesus' life was seasoned with prayer In the truest sense, Christ is the greatest Example of prayer in the greatest Book on prayer. His very name is the crux of all prayer. Weekly His name stops wheels of commerce, silences our halls of justice, empties our universities, and locks industry's mighty doors. When Sunday arrives millions enter temples of worship, cathedrals of Christianity, mud huts of praise, and brush arbors of prayer, all because of Jesus.

Much has been said of the power of prayer. Volumes have discussed the force of prayer. Sermons have stressed the need for prayer. People have proven the value of prayer. But were it not for Jesus' name, prayerful lips would be sealed in deathlike silence. When one really prays in His name, intelligently and scripturally, it is as though Christ Himself prayed. To the sinner, Jesus' name means forgiveness. To the sick, His name means healing. To the lonely, His name means comfort. To the pray-er, His name means power.

Prayer's trail at last has led to the Source of all power. Upon the lofty peak at the end of the Road of Prayer we see the cross of Jesus. Were it not for this cross, prayer would be altogether useless. Had it not been for John's four powerful words, "and bearing his cross," prayer would hold no impact. Yet, because of Jesus' name there is no force, might, or authority on earth that can prevent prayer's answer. Those who learn to kneel in humility and weakness will soon feel God's supernatural power. The man of prayer is the man of power.

> We kneel — and all about us seems to
>   lower;
> We rise — and all, the distant and the
>   near,
> Stands forth in sunny outline, brave and
>   clear.
> We kneel, how weak! We rise, how full
>   of power!
> — Richard Chenevix Trench

APPENDIX: PRACTICAL PRAYING

To pray in a practical, systematic manner, the prayer warrior needs two things: something to pray about during his or her prayer time, and a quiet place to pray, a place where uninterrupted intercession can be offered for needs of the world. To make your prayer more practical consider these two areas of thought.

How to pray

God gives you 96 fifteen-minute time periods every day. Will you give God at least one or two of these time periods in prayer for your loved ones, friends, and the world? Some, of course, do not respond because they lack a workable method in their prayer life. Some say, "I let the Holy Spirit lead," and when asked how much prayer the Holy Spirit led them into during the last week, they blush with embarrassment. Indeed, why must we wait for a call today when God's Word cries out to all generations: "Pray without ceasing" (I Thess. 5:17). Thus we have a constant call, and to be obedient to that call, we must answer. That is why we offer the reader several hints on how to pray. . . .

First, divide your fifteen-minute time period into three periods. The first five-minute period could be given to praise, adoration and worship of the Lord. Take time to love God because He is God. Remember, the way to enter the gates of heaven is thanksgiving and praise (Ps. 100). After this you will be ready to pray for other needs.

Second, take five minutes to pray for needs that are close to you. This could mean prayer for family concerns as well as for your local area, including your church and pastor. You will be surprised how much can be included in a five-minute prayer time.

Finally, pray for specific countries of the world (W.L.C. offices have prayer maps available on request to all interested prayer warriors. These maps show the location of all countries as well as their names). Since there are 210 separate geographical areas we call countries, to name all 210 in five minutes would mean mere mention of each country. Our suggestion is to either extend your prayer time or divide the 210 countries into thirty countries each, each day lifting thirty of the countries before God. Thus, every seven days you will be praying for the whole world.

But what can we pray about concerning these many obscure places? For one thing, most certainly follow the command of Jesus to pray that the Lord of harvest will send forth laborers into the harvest (Matt. 9:38). We should also ask God for the conversion of souls in each country, since His Word declares, "Ask of the heathen for thine inheritance" (Ps. 2:8). Further, pray that God will bless the efforts of World Literature Crusade distribution (involving Christians of 415 denominations) in that specific geographic area. A sample prayer might be as follows: "Oh, God, I lift before you Indonesia. I claim the precious souls of this country for my inheritance. Please send forth laborers into the harvest of Indonesia, and bless those ministers presently carrying forth the gospel throughout Indonesia. Place a special anointing on the daily efforts of World Literature Crusade men as they attempt to reach every home with the gospel in many villages today."

The above prayer requires less than twenty seconds and yet calls to God on behalf of that nation. Even if the prayer warrior only mentions the country in but a passing prayer, God will honor such intercession. Of course, in all of this we must covet the precious leading of God's Spirit. He will often prompt us to stop and pray more carefully for a certain country. And remember, when calling on God in behalf of Communist and Moslem nations, be sure to ask God that leaders in the highest levels of these governments will experience changes of attitude so doors will open for an anointed systematic distribution of the gospel to all the people of these countries. (All registered prayer partners with World Literature Crusade receive specific requests for the world on a frequent basis).

Where to pray

Following several years in which God showed this author the impact and value of prayer, he was jolted one night by a startling vision of a prayer center where college-age youth could come from across the country to offer God a gift of time set aside as an offering of intercession. During the year of their commitment these dedicated youth would pray at least two hours a day, praying in specific, assigned time periods so that prayer would never stop day or night at that center. The specific room where these young people would pray was to be called "The Gap," based on God's words to Ezekiel, "I sought for a man among them that should make up the hedge and stand in the gap before me for the land . . ." (Ezek. 22:30). Six months after the evening of this challenging vision, God gave us our prayer center. For years prayer has continued day and night in "The Gap" at this prayer center. Many miracles have resulted from this prayer, not the least of which is the spreading of the "gap concept." Today, hundreds of families, churches, and colleges have begun a gap ministry by setting aside a specific place called "The Gap," where people can pray for the needs of the world.

To my knowledge, the first couple to ever begin a gap

ministry in the home as the result of hearing about our prayer center were from a Baptist background. Since that time people from many denominations have written us saying, "Add us to your "gap" list! We've begun a family prayer ministry in our home."

My wife Dee and myself have started our own family gap ministry. We had a special family prayer chapel built in our back yard where we could go individually or together for prayer and devotions. It has revolutionized my personal prayer life. Each day I pray for the countries of the world in our gap. What a thrill to hear our two daughters Dena and Ginger, only six and three years of age, beg us to go to "the gap" to hear about Jesus and pray. They invariably want me to tell them about different countries of the world on the globe, one of the few objects of furniture in our gap.

To begin a gap ministry, one must simply set aside a closet or spare room for a place of prayer. Our family saved the necessary money to put down an inexpensive piece of carpet and to panel the walls of our gap so the atmosphere would be conducive to quiet prayer. Of course, the most important thing is a special place reserved just for prayer. Our gap is not a sewing room, den, or office that doubles as a prayer chapel. Every family member knows it is our special "Gethsemane" where we can retreat to be alone with our Lord. I challenge the reader to start a gap ministry soon and register your gap ministry with our World Literature Crusade gap list.

Direct all requests for further information to:

Dick Eastman
Change the World School of Prayer
Box 1313
Studio City, CA 91604

BIBLIOGRAPHY

Allen, Charles L., *All Things Are Possible Through Prayer.* Old Tappan, N.J.: Fleming H. Revell, 1958

Bounds, Edward M., *Purpose in Prayer.* Chicago: Moody Press, n.d.

_____, *Power through Prayer.* Grand Rapids: Zondervan, n.d.

Gordon, Samuel D., *Quiet Talks on Prayer.* New York: Grosset and Dunlap, 1904

Grubb, Norman P., *Rees Howells: Intercessor.* Fort Washington, Pa.: Christian Literature Crusade, 1962

Huegel, F. J., *Prayer's Deeper Secrets.* Grand Rapids: Zondervan, 1959

Laubach, Frank C., *Prayer, the Mightiest Force in the World.* Old Tappan, N.J.: Fleming H. Revell, 1959

Lawrence, Brother, *Practice of the Presence of God.* Old Tappan, N.J.: Fleming H. Revell, 1956

Lawson, J. Gilchrist, *Deeper Experiences of Famous Christians.* Anderson, Ind.: Warner Press, 1911

McGraw, Francis A., *Praying Hyde.* Chicago: Moody Press, n.d.

Payne, Thomas, *Prayer — the Greatest Force on Earth.* Chicago: Moody Press, n.d.

Sims, A., ed., *George Müller: Man of Faith.* Chicago: Moody Press, n.d.

Spurgeon, Charles H., *Effective Prayer.* London: The Evangelical Press, n.d.

Steere, Douglas V., *Dimensions of Prayer.* New York: Harper & Row, 1963

Unknown, *The Kneeling Christian.* Grand Rapids, Zondervan, 1945